# PLAYS BY
# PHIL BOSAKOWSKI

**BROADWAY PLAY PUBLISHING INC**
56 E 81st St., NY NY 10028-0202
212 772-8334  fax: 212 772-8358
http://www.BroadwayPlayPubl.com

PLAYS BY PHIL BOSAKOWSKI
© Copyright 1999 by the estate of Phil Bosakowski

First printing: March 2000
ISBN: 0-88145-165-7

Book design: Marie Donovan
Word processing: Microsoft Word for Windows
Typographic controls: Xerox Ventura Publisher 2.0 PE
Typeface: Palatino
Copy editing: Jonathan Mindes
Printed on recycled acid-free paper and bound in the U S A

# CONTENTS

# INTRODUCTION

Truly funny plays that not only make you laugh out loud—even in the reading—but also make you think for a long time about such big and varied topics as passion, politics and history, deserve to be kept alive. This new publication of three of Phil Bosakowski's plays, the first appearance in print of his last play, NIXON APOLOGIZES TO THE NATION, helps assure that longevity. Highly adventurous and eminently theatrical, these plays are more like cubist paintings with musical accompaniments than literature intended to be read. The texts were written to be played, and for the fullest experience they must be—even if only by actors moving around with a few props. But the solitary act of reading them also has its rewards in the fun and detailed exposure to Phil's comic voice and compassionate world view. His humor, outrage and sense of American history combine and reconfigure in ways that surprise and unsettle our complacency, challenging us to look afresh at our history, our figureheads and ourselves. This is humor with an edge, but it doesn't bite viciously. Phil's hearty satire borrows from Monty Python and the Marx Brothers to goad us out of our grudges.

With BIERCE (1974) Phil looks at political chicanery in late nineteenth century America through the hard-edged and steady gaze of the journalist Ambrose Bierce. The speed of the story and the concision of its characters, as if carved by a scalpel, push the play's realism to its very limits. With CHOPIN (1984) Phil bursts out of that realism and revels in the discovery that he can do anything on stage, anything! In his introductory notes Phil says, "Think Monty Python. That absolute commitment to unlikely reality." German tanks invade Poland when Hitler's drawings of tanks get clipped to a clothesline that rolls across the stage. Tormented by The Bear/Russia, Chopin/Lech Welesa goes to Washington and finds himself in Duck Soup. F D R on ukelele acts like Groucho and Eleanor Roosevelt on the slide trombone like Margaret Dumont, in cahoots with the silent Russian Bear who beeps Harpo's horn. With NIXON (1994) Phil combines the two approaches, wrapping the realistic line of development around a surreal free-for-all. In ten takes facing the television cameras Nixon tries to tape an apology to the nation, takes which momentarily stall and inevitably provoke the eruptions of Nixon's warped visions of people and events in American history. He, Nixon, is that baby born of the love that cannot speak its name between Walt Whitman and George Washington. In his Uncle Sam costume that he sewed himself Nixon courts Emily Dickinson on Halloween, trick or treating at her house with sidekicks J Edgar Hoover (in a dress of course) and J F K (who would rather be hitting up a sorority house). Later his Pat Nixon/Emily Dickinson First Lady can be induced to leave her solitary retreat in an upstairs room only with the lie that he will retire from politics and return to California.

Phil wrote BIERCE TAKES ON THE RAILROAD! in the early 1970s while still a university student at Villanova. The College of Marin's Theatre III gave the play its first full production, with the then unknown Robin Williams playing William Randolph Hearst. Another production took place at Iowa University where Phil earned an M F A in playwriting and wrote on sports for the local newspaper. In 1973 pioneer American dramaturg, Arthur H Ballet, edited and published BIERCE in *Playwrights for Tomorrow*. That was an earlier version of BIERCE than the one which appears in this volume. In both versions Hearst's opening speech tells us what the play is about: "...a country. My country. The United States of America as she used to be. As we moved from the nineteenth to the twentieth century.... They were doing the Two-Step then. And the Cakewalk. And the Turkey Trot." On assignment for Hearst'spaper, Bierce leaves California for Senate hearings in Washington where he stands up to the Pacific Western Railroad, Mark Twain, and Teddy Roosevelt. While Pancho Villa waits for Bierce and their shootout in Mexico, Bierce's gun gets turned on his son. "Nothing matters. Everything matters."

A decade later, following some years in San Francisco working with the Bay Area Playwrights, Phil returned to New York City and wrote CHOPIN IN SPACE. Midwestern Playlabs helped with play development, and then Yale Repertory under the artistic leadership of Lloyd Richards fully produced it. The play opened at The Ark in New York City in May of 1985 to critical acclaim in the *New York Times* and the *Voice*. This is the play's fourth publication following Yale *Theatre*, Dramatists Play Service, and P A J's *Wordplays 4*. In his unpublished papers Phil gives this brief synopsis: "Frederick Chopin is hounded to do something wonderful for his native Poland. Should he make music? Become a patriot named Lech Walesa? Or what? A romp through two hundred years of Polish history, with guest appearances by Franklin Roosevelt, Adolph Hitler, George Sand and the Pope."

This is the first publication of Phil's last play, NIXON APOLOGIZES TO THE NATION. Workshopped at the Playwrights Center in Minneapolis in 1991 and then further developed and staged the following year at Denver Center Theatre Company's U S West Fest, NIXON became a finalist in Actors Theatre of Louisville's Great American Play Contest. But it was only after Phil's death that the play received a full production, at Wesleyan University, with Remy Auberjonois playing Nixon. A benefit performance at Wesleyan raised money for Hospice at Middlesex Hospital where Phil died from pancreatic cancer in September 1994. Again, here is Phil's own description of the play: "Alone in The Oval Office as his lease on the

Presidency shortens, Dick Nixon, all-American, wonders where the fuck he went wrong. Was it when he chopped down that cherry tree and lied about it? When he went trick or treating with J F K and J Edgar Hoover? Or was it that Checkers Speech?" Phil's first notion of a play about Nixon began in a tiny laundromat near the Mouffetard in Paris. Staring at the dryer he told me he wanted to explore what he loved and what he hated about America. At that time (Gulf War 1991) Phil was still part of a comedy writing team providing Garrison Keillor with material for his radio show. Phil wrote a short bit about a laundromat that we hand delivered to Garrison for his London debut. But the radio voices that Phil started hearing in that French laundromat were not Garrison's, but Amos 'n Andy's. Something about a videotape in their family heirlooms that had a shot of Lincoln's assassination, casting some doubt on the tradition of Booth in the booth. The ride had begun! As he wrote (he was working at the same time on an opera libretto about Betty Boop) he kept getting interrupted by Richard Nixon, and it was only after some resistance that Phil gave in and let Nixon come out center stage. What had started out as something about a 1940s radio show with white actors imitating black dialects duping the listeners into thinking they were tuned into black culture, became with Nixon a bigger play about a country grown too comfortable with duplicity. Phil finished his third and final "polish" of NIXON APOLOGIZES TO THE NATION two months before he was diagnosed with cancer. In those last few months of his life he sketched out a play with three characters, all dead, a comedy team writing jokes for a show about how they died, all three having had the same disease (pancreatic cancer): Hrostwitha a ninth century German nun, Molière the seventeenth century French actor/playwright, and Bosakowski the twentieth century American teacher/writer. Maybe in the future some waggish playwright in some laundromat will hear what they've come up with and spin out a good rewrite.

Gay Smith

# ABOUT THE AUTHOR

PHIL BOSAKOWSKI
(1946-1994)

Born November 1, 1946, Passaic, New Jersey

1946-65 Grew up in Garfield, Clifton, and Trenton, New Jersey; parents
Frank Bosakowski and Emily Pirog, brothers Paul and James, sister Mary.
Early visits to Ukrainian and Polish grandparents in Manhattan's Lower
East Side, setting for his film script *How I Got My Apartment*; and subject
for his unfinished play POLACKS ON PARADE; Sixth grade Phil played
George Washington at St Brendan's School, Clifton, NJ. In Trenton public
high school he starred in DIARY OF ANNE FRANK, wrote for school paper.

1969 BA in English, Villanova University

1970 MA in Theater, Villanova University
Shubert Fellowship 1970

1969-72 Director of Theater at Harcum Junior College, PA
GENESIS! at Cafe LaMama

1972 BIERCE TAKES ON THE RAILROAD!
First produced at College of Marin's Theater III with Robin Williams
playing William Randolph Hearst. Published by Arthur H Ballet in
anthology *Playwrights for Tomorrow, Volume II* (U of Minnesota Press)

1972-75 M F A in Playwriting, University of Iowa
Editor *Daily Iowan*
Norman Felton Fellowship 1973

1976-1984 New Dramatists; Teaching Playwriting for Actors
LEADING OFF AND PLAYING SHORTSTOP at Berkeley Stage Company,
CA

1980 N E A Award
Director, Playwrights Workshop, University of Iowa
THE FLOOD produced at Wilkes College Center, PA

1981 MINSTREL SHOW at Bay Area Playwrights, Marin Co., CA

1982 PALM 90 at Bay Area Playwrights in collaboration with Sherry
Kramer, Jeff Jones and Gilbert Girion
KIDS AND DOGS reading at New Dramatists

1983 Midwest Play Labs, Minneapolis, MN
Two weeks in Poland through auspices of New Dramatists
DISAPPEARING ACTS reading at Florida Studio Theater
DISAPPEARING ACTS production at Raft Theater, N Y C

1983-1992 Dramaturg and Moderator/Teacher for Florida Studio Theater's
New Play Festivals

1984 CHOPIN IN SPACE, Yale Repertory, January
CHOPIN published in *Word Plays 4*, P A J
CHOPIN published in Yale *Theater*
University of Iowa Playwrights Workshop Festival
Professor/Resident Playwright for Perserverence Theater and University of
Alaska, Juneau
Bay Area Playwrights Festival. Co-director
Playwright in Residence, Florida Studio Theater
DOUGLAS ON FIRE (later titled BUSTER COMES THROUGH!) reading at
Playwrights Horizons

1984-1991 Playwriting Teacher, Warren Hills Arts Symposium, Washington,
NJ (high school and junior high students)

1984-1990 Phil helps Casey Childs found Primary Stages
He teaches Playwriting Workshops for Primary Stages
KIDS AND DOGS and other P B scripts read at Primary Stages

1985 CHOPIN IN SPACE at Ark Theater, N Y C
Reading of CHOPIN at Theater Works, L A
Playwright in Residence, New West Productions, Boise, Idaho

1986 HOME STREET HOME, Theater for a New Audience, N Y C
New York Foundation for the Arts Award
Collaboration on screen play with Adam Holender
CHOPIN IN SPACE published by Dramatists Play Service

1987 OUR GOD'S BROTHER , Phil's adaptation of Karol Wojtyla's
(Pope John Paul II) play, reading at Detroit's Attic Theater
Director, Playwrights Workshop, University of Iowa
CROSSIN' THE LINE at Delaware Theater Company, commissioned by
Delaware State Bar Association
Elected to Polish Institute of Arts and Sciences
S W A P reading (later titled WHEEL AND DEAL), New Arts at The
Knitting Factory

1987-93 Professor of Screen Writing, Film Department, School for the Visual
Arts

1988 CROSSIN' THE LINE published by Dramatists Play Service
NORMAL-C at Cal State University at Chico; Professor/Playwright in
Residence

WHEEL AND DEAL, New Arts Theater Co. at the Garage
N E A Award
Volunteer, East Harlem Tutorial Program

1989 CROSSIN' THE LINE at Lamb's Theater, N Y C
Teacher/Director of Dramatic Writing, Cal State University Summer School
for the Arts
Professor/Resident Playwright, Dartmouth College
Volunteer, Harlem Hospital Border Babies

1990-91 Writer for Garrison Keillor's American Radio Company

1990 BUSTER COMES THROUGH! staged reading at the O'Neill National
Playwrights Conference

1991 Three months residence in Paris, France
HOW I GOT MY APARTMENT screen play reading at the O'Neill National
Playwrights Conference
Winner of Herbert and Patricia Brodkin Award at the O'Neill Conference
BETTY AT THE KOOL KLUB, book for one-act opera about Betty Boop,
music Catherine Stone; Overtone Theater, Mill Valley, CA
McKnight Fellowship, Playwrights Center, Minn., reading of first draft of
NIXON APOLOGIZES TO THE NATION
52nd Street Project. Ensemble Studio Theater
U S O PLAYS THE SANDS; Cabaret Salute to the Kids in Khaki Fighting the
Iraqui, New Arts, Samuel Beckett Theater, N Y C

1992 BUSTER COMES THROUGH! staged reading at Denver Center
Theater Company's US West Theater Fest
Professor/Resident Playwright, Princeton University
52nd Street Project, Ensemble Studio Theater
Dramaturg for the O'Neill National Playwrights Conference

1993 NIXON APOLOGIZES TO THE NATION staged reading at Denver
Center Theater Co.'s US West Theater Fest
Marries Gay (Manifold) Smith at the O'Neill Theater Center, residence in
Portland, CT and N Y C
Director of W P A, Wesleyan University Playwrights Advancement
Dramaturg for the O'Neill National Playwrights Conference

1994 Professor/Playwright, Wesleyan University
Diagnosed with pancreatic cancer in May

Died September 11, 1994, Middletown, CT

1995 NIXON APOLOGIZES TO THE NATION produced at Wesleyan
University. Benefit performance for Hospice Unit at Middlesex Hospital
in Middletown, CT

September 18th,1995, PHIL BOSAKOWSKI THEATER dedication at
Primary Stages, New York City

PLAYS BY PHIL BOSAKOWSKI

Annual BUG N' BUB PLAYWRIGHTS SCHOLARSHIP FUND AWARD
in memory of Phil to a playwright with a daring comic voice and sense of
anarchy and play: Mark Eisner 1995, Kira Obolensky 1996, Gordon
Dahlquist 1997, David Abaire 1998, Kelly Stuart 1999

# BIERCE TAKES ON THE RAILROAD!

# ORIGINAL PRODUCTION

BIERCE TAKES ON THE RAILROAD! was first presented at College of
Marin on 20 July 1972. The cast and creative contributors were:

WILLIAM RANDOLPH HEARST . . . . . . . . . . . . . . . . . . . . . . . . . . . . .Robin Williams
HARTFORD T KENT . . . . . . . . . . . . . . . . . . . . . . . . . . . . . . . . . . . J W Harper
AMBROSE BIERCE . . . . . . . . . . . . . . . . . . . . . . . . . . . . . . . . . Kurtwood Smith
MOLLIE BIERCE . . . . . . . . . . . . . . . . . . . . . . . . . . . . . . . . . . Charline Sutton
DAY BIERCE . . . . . . . . . . . . . . . . . . . . . . . . . . . . . . . . . . . . . . . . .Craig Scott
LEIGH BIERCE . . . . . . . . . . . . . . . . . . . . . . . . . . . . . . . . . . Marc Hildebrand
ROGER MERTON . . . . . . . . . . . . . . . . . . . . . . . . . . . . . . . . . . . . Alan Kernan
EMILY WILTON . . . . . . . . . . . . . . . . . . . . . . . . . . . . . . . Carolyn Reed-Dunn
PANCHO VILLA . . . . . . . . . . . . . . . . . . . . . . . . . . . . . . . . . . . Robert Cooper
CHORUS . . . . . . . . . . . . . . . . . Lisa Beasley, Abby Goldman, Marc Hildebrand
Kendall Jackson, Anni Long, Rich Shanower
David Silverman, Kent Skov, W H Teed

*Director* . . . . . . . . . . . . . . . . . . . . . . . . . . . . . . . . . . . . . . . . . . . . . . .James Dunn

# CHARACTERS & SETTING

TEDDY ROOSEVELT, *President of the United States*
ROGER MERTON, *Senator from Ohio*
AMBROSE BIERCE, *a crusading journalist*
WILLIAM RANDOLPH HEARST, *a young publisher*
HARTFORD T KENT, *a railroad tycoon*
MARK TWAIN, *an American legend*
LEIGH BIERCE, *a young man*
MAGGIE, *a railroad widow*
EMILY WILTON, *a Washington party-giver*
PANCHO VILLA, *the Mexican revolutionary*

CHORUS, *eight men and women who serve as Congressmen, journalists, and concerned citizens*


*The action takes place at the turn of the last century, in the United States of America.*

# ACT ONE

HEARST: Bierce takes on the railroad! This play is not my story. It's not about William Randolph Hearst. Bierce takes on the railroad. That's the story. It's about Ambrose Gwinnet Bierce, the Devil's Disciple, who worked for me. And a railroad. That I fought tooth and nail. And a paper. *The San Francisco Examiner*, the Monarch of the Dailies. My paper. My first paper. But that's another story.

And it's about a country. My country. The United States of America, as she used to be. As we moved from the nineteenth to the twentieth century. My country. When we were young. And strong. Before we remembered the Maine, and a bit afterwards. But that's neither here nor there. Ambrose Bierce takes on the railroad! It's a play of the times, brought to you by the greatest of newspapers. Extra! Extra! Read all about it! They were doing the Two-Step then. And the Cakewalk. And the Turkey Trot. They were innocent. And gullible. And they were buying newspapers. My newspapers. And they believed in what America stood for. And they believed in what I stood for. Why, America and I stood for the same things!

(HEARST *puts a record on the Victrola, cranks it up, and* KENT, MERTON *and the* CHORUS *dance on.*)

KENT: Good evening, gentlemen of the Senate!

CHORUS: Good evening, Mr Kent.

KENT: I imagine you know why I've called you here today. It's a little matter concerning my railroad.

CHORUS: Yes, sir! God bless the Pacific Western.

HEARST: God bless the Pacific Western! But not everyone was blessing it. My reporters were there. Bierce was there.

(BIERCE, *accompanied by* LEIGH, *meet* MAGGIE *across from* KENT *and* CHORUS.)

MAGGIE: This is where it happened, Mr Bierce. Matthew was standing here, Betty's husband was over there, the Carson brothers, some men from Bad Coon River. The railroad men over there, guns and horses.

BIERCE: Were they armed?

MAGGIE: The railroad men had guns.

BIERCE: Your husband and the others?

MAGGIE: Jimmy Carson had a shovel. We couldn't pay five cents a pound to ship our wheat.

LEIGH: This is railroad property.

MAGGIE: It's where Matthew got shot.

*(Cut to* KENT *et al)*

KENT: Gentlemen of the Senate: the United States government has helped us make our country the great nation it is today. Needless to say, the Pacific Western has been fortunate, too.

CHORUS: Anything for progress, Mr Kent.

KENT: Yes, yes, yes indeed. You all remember that, and I shall, too. But the railroad has got to expand with the country. Now, Senator—

MERTON: Merton.

KENT: Senator Merton, from Ohio? Used to be a trip from Ohio to San Francisco'd take months. Now it's less than a week, and we can do better. Three days! Boys, the people of America deserve a railroad as good as they are, as great as they are, as big as they are. But let's get particular. *(He pulls out an orange.)* Oranges, gentlemen: Like to see them on every table in the country, every month of the year. Fresh, cheap, and good for you. We can deliver oranges at Christmas, as soon as we lay the track. If we had the money. Which is where you gentlemen can help. We may not be able to repay the Funding Bill just now.

CHORUS #1: So, Mr Kent, you'd see an advantage to our re-funding the railroad.

KENT: Your words, Senator. We'd repay every cent, maybe when the P W's reached full growth.

CHORUS #2: And about when would that be, Mr Kent?

KENT: Our lawyers can go over the details. I have no head for figures. Heh-heh.

CHORUS: Heh-heh.

*(Cut to* BIERCE *et al)*

BIERCE: What did they do, ma'am, Matthew and the others.

MAGGIE: They blocked the tracks.

BIERCE: And the agents were called?

MAGGIE: They were there. They were looking for trouble.

LEIGH: The law would say your Matthew was trespassing.

MAGGIE: The law says you can't shoot a man in the back. I come to you for help, Mr Bierce.

BIERCE: There's nothing I can do for you, my good woman.

MAGGIE: You can tell his story, Mr Bierce.

*(Cut to* KENT *et al)*

KENT: Gentlemen, I say let's do business for America in the American way. No need to make a federal case out of it. Heh-heh.

CHORUS #4: That's good, a federal case.

MERTON: Mr Kent, I've heard reports of farmers protesting shipping rates who were attacked by your railroad agents, and that some were shot dead.

KENT: At Mussel Slough. A sad event, Senator, but the road was not at fault. It's conditions today. You ought to speak to your colleagues from our state.

MERTON: Where are they now?

KENT: Inspecting the great railroads of Europe and Asia, at no expense to the taxpayer, I might add. Gentlemen, the Pacific Western Railroad wants to keep up with America. So America can keep up with the world.

CHORUS #3: I'm for progress.

KENT: And I'm for you. Ever see a gold spike? Got a few back here, little mementos, keep your boys' ties in place, and a little something for the lady at home to put in her hair. Commemorate our progress.

MERTON: Gentlemen, I propose a hearing to consider this proposal. People have been shot at. We're talking about murder, land theft, mineral rights, deferring money the public loaned the railroad in good faith—

KENT: Excuse me, Senator Merton, I haven't finished. The people of California are good and hard-working people. The railroad serves them well. Certainly we have had some minor problems, but can you blame us if some people, some factions and elements, want to impugn our integrity? It's conditions today, bad conditions that are getting worse. Conditions that create factions, who are against progress, free enterprise, and the railroad. I am a humble man, and my great railroad is humble. I can't pick up a staff like Moses and say to California "Come, follow me!" There will be dissenters, and there is a place for them in our great state. If they don't like the way we do business, let them build their own railroad. We'd welcome the competition.

CHORUS #4: That's good enough for me.

CHORUS #5: Me, too.

CHORUS: And me...and me...and me.

CHORUS #2: Mr Kent, I don't know the conditions in California, but if you think it's good for the country and good for business, I'll take your word for it.

MERTON: Gentlemen, I propose we take no action on the bill until the farmers—

CHORUS #2: If the farmers have something to say, they know where to find us. Mr Kent, thank you for coming here.

KENT: Gentlemen, I see a great day ahead for American enterprise.

MERTON: Mr Kent, I object! Mr Kent!

(KENT *exits, followed by* MERTON.)

HEARST: Bierce takes on the railroad! It's a play of the times. It's his story. It's America's story. And it's your story. Me, I'm just a simple newspaper publisher by the name of Hearst, trying to bring you the story—

CHORUS: That's right!

HEARST: Not yet! —trying to bring you the story just the way it happened. The news. But first a song for Ambrose Bierce, the Devil's Disciple. His song for America.

CHORUS #1: Get in place, everyone get in place.

(*The* CHORUS *lines up for song.*)

CHORUS: My country 'tis of thee,
Sweet land of felony,
Of thee I sing—
Land where my fathers fried
Young witches and applied
Whips to the Quakers' hides
And made them spring.

(BIERCE *sits at his typewriter and begins typing.*)

CHORUS #8: Is that really what's-his-name?

CHORUS #2: Quiet!

CHORUS #3: He's working.

CHORUS #1: Look at him.

CHORUS #2: The fool.

CHORUS #7: Who cares?

CHORUS #3: He cares.

CHORUS #4: Who cares about him?

CHORUS #3: I don't care.

CHORUS #5: Hey, good news!

CHORUS: What?

CHORUS #5: We're going on a new job.

CHORUS #1: New job?

CHORUS #5: Yeah.

CHORUS #1: What is it?

CHORUS #5: The boss'll tell you.

CHORUS #2: Boss here?

CHORUS #8: Hearst? You mean Hearst's going to give Bierce a new job?

CHORUS #6: W R Hearst offers A G Bierce a new job! But he's got a job.

CHORUS #4: The Devil's Disciple. He's out to spite the world.

CHORUS #2: No, he's after bigger fish than that.

CHORUS #8: Why is Mr Hearst going to give Mr Bierce a new job?

CHORUS #5: Because Mr Hearst is angry at the railroad. He says Ambrose is going to do something about it.

CHORUS #3: What can Ambrose do?

CHORUS #4: What can Ambrose do? Don't you know who Ambrose Gwinnet Bierce is? A G Bierce?

CHORUS #1: Bierce?

CHORUS #2: Bierce!

CHORUS #5: Bierce?

CHORUS #4: Bierce!

CHORUS #5: Bierce?

CHORUS #6: Bierce!

CHORUS #7: Bierce?

CHORUS #8: Bierce!

CHORUS #4: The A G stands for Almighty God.

CHORUS #1: Don't let him hear you say that.

CHORUS #4: Why?

CHORUS #1: He carries a gun.

CHORUS #4: Nothing matters.

CHORUS #1: If he's stood up against a wall in Mexico and shot to rags, he'll think it's a pretty good way to leave this world.

PANCHO VILLA: *(Entering)* Hey! Hombre! You want to come to Mexico? Maybe join up with Pancho Villa, great bandit of the West? I give you a close shave. No shit.

CHORUS #2: To be a gringo in Mexico—ah, that is euthanasia!

PANCHO VILLA: Okay, hombre, I be seeing you later. Later. *(He exits.)*

CHORUS #4: Nothing matters.

CHORUS #7: Here's the boss. Everybody get busy.

*(HEARST enters.)*

HEARST: Stand up straight! Get to work! Stop talking! Straighten that tie! Shine those shoes! Look sharp! Nothing to do? You're fired!

CHORUS: Yes sir...yes sir...yes sir...thank you, sir.

HEARST: Mr Bierce, may I speak to you a moment?

BIERCE: You are speaking to me, Mr Hearst.

HEARST: I have something I'd like to discuss with you.

BIERCE: Another crusade, Mr Hearst?

HEARST: Crusade?

BIERCE: What is it this time? Are we going to unionize the dead, give women the vote or house the Chinese in San Francisco Bay?

HEARST: Bierce, what do you think of Hartford T Kent?

BIERCE: The man should be used as a decoy in shooting matches.

HEARST: Bierce, he's in Washington.

BIERCE: He's in Washington because his railroad owes the government seventy-five million dollars. Naturally, he does not intend to pay back a cent. He wants to postpone the payment for eighty years. Is that what you wanted to tell me?

HEARST: The thing'll pass, Bierce.

BIERCE: Of course it will pass. He owns every vote in the West. The paper should have someone covering those hearings, Mr Hearst. A man telling the truth about the Pacific Western Railroad.

HEARST: Think so?

BIERCE: But, nothing matters.

HEARST: Bierce, "Nothing matters" doesn't fill a newspaper. We need angles, something to make people sit up and say this is wrong! And I read about it in the Hearst paper! A couple of farmers got shot. Cold-blooded murder!

BIERCE: To attack Kent for shooting farmers is merely to attack his discretion. To expose his corruption, to prove him lying under oath about railroad finances, is to attack his credibility. You write the headlines, Mr Hearst, and I will write the copy.

HEARST: Bierce, I'm sending you to Washington to represent the state and beat this thing. We'll build a campaign, a big campaign, we'll write letters, sign petitions, hold rallies, fight hard for truth and justice! We're going to break the railroad's hold on California.

BIERCE: And we are going to sell newspapers and hurry you along to Sacramento, and then maybe to the White House, on a white horse. Good for you, Mr Hearst.

HEARST: We are going to loosen the railroad's grasp on this great state. What sounds good? California shakes the shackles of corporate bondage! State says no to corporate powers! This is something the governor should have done! Bierce, this is front page stuff. I'm making you the hope of California!

BIERCE: All that on twenty-five dollars a week?

HEARST: Ambrose Bierce, the People's Hope! I'll raise it to an even fifty.

BIERCE: Mr Hearst, the abolition of Hell has deprived me of hope. Nevertheless, for sixty dollars I shall go to Washington.

HEARST: And I thought hope was cheap. I thought nothing mattered.

BIERCE: Nothing does matter. Money eases that knowledge.

HEARST: When can you leave?

BIERCE: Immediately.

HEARST: That's too soon. Leave first thing in the morning. After the rally.

BIERCE: If you insist.

HEARST: Hot damn! Stop the presses!

CHORUS #1: Stop the presses!

CHORUS #6: Extra! Extra! Stop the presses!

CHORUS #2: Why bother?

CHORUS #4: Extra! Extra! Read all about it! Read all about it! Hearst launches attack on the railroad!

HEARST: Make that Mister Hearst.

CHORUS #1: Mister Hearst sets out to break Pacific Western's hold on our state!

CHORUS #3: He outlines a plan of action!

CHORUS #7: Monster railroad to lose its death grip—

HEARST: Make that "tyrant railroad"!

CHORUS #7: Tyrant railroad to lose its death grip on our state!

CHORUS #8: Read how William Randolph Hearst will crush railroad's back! He tells us what private citizens can do!

CHORUS #2: *San Francisco Examiner* to fight Railroad Funding Bill! They will send a representative to Washington!

HEARST: Try one with octopus.

CHORUS #6: Fearless young editor takes on the octopus: Read all about it!

HEARST: I like that.

CHORUS #2: Three cheers for Mr Hearst!

HEARST: I like that.

CHORUS: Hip-hip...hurrah! Hip-hip...hurrah! Hip-hip...hurrah!

CHORUS #6: William Randolph Hearst for governor!

HEARST: I hear America singing. Ladies and gentlemen, we are going to bring good government back to California. We are going to clean out the cellar of corruption and move to an attic of clean government!

CHORUS: *(Carrying* HEARST *off.)* Hurrah for Mister Hearst! He'll save our state!

CHORUS #4: *(Exiting)* Extra! Extra! Read about how William Randolph Hearst plans to strip the Pacific Western of its death hold on our state. He announces his plans at a rally tonight! Come early!

BIERCE: The People's Hope.

PANCHO VILLA: Sí. The People's Hope.

BIERCE: Nationally syndicated. After thirty years of writing for no one in San Francisco, now to be writing for no one nationally.

PANCHO VILLA: Señor, nothing matters.

BIERCE: What if this matters? What if I fail? What if no one takes up my cause? I know I'm right. Who else knows?

PANCHO VILLA: Señor, nothing matters.

BIERCE: Nothing matters.

*(*LEIGH *and* MAGGIE *enter across stage.)*

LEIGH: See, the way it should've been handled was, you and your people are standing there, just standing there. Hi, Mr Railroad Agent Man, nice day.

Private property? How about that? I got some private property for you. *(He pulls out his father's gun.)* And then bam! They want to mix it up? Bam! Bam!

MAGGIE: We didn't know.

LEIGH: You should've.

BIERCE: What are you doing with my gun, Leigh?

LEIGH: I was showing it to Maggie.

MAGGIE: Wish we had a couple of them.

BIERCE: Would your friend excuse us?

LEIGH: Maggie?

MAGGIE: I'm not going to wait around all day. *(Exits)*

BIERCE: A gun is not a toy, Leigh. It is an instrument used to kill people.

LEIGH: I know.

BIERCE: Good.

LEIGH: Can I have it?

BIERCE: Do you intend to kill someone?

LEIGH: No.

BIERCE: Then lower it, please. Thank you. I am leaving for Washington, Leigh.

LEIGH: I thought you were going to join up with Pancho Villa.

BIERCE: Not until I oppose the Funding Bill. For Mr Hearst.

LEIGH: Hearst! He's just using you to hurry himself to Sacramento, and then maybe to the White House. But nothing matters.

BIERCE: That is what I intend to find out in Washington. If perhaps, maybe, this could matter. When I was a young man, Leigh, on my birthday, I would challenge my Uncle Ephraim to an arm-wrestling contest. I would run to his house after dinner and announce, "Today I am sixteen (or whatever) and man enough to beat you." At his game, Leigh. And he would scowl, and look me right in the eye, and I would try to match his look. And then he'd scowl some more, roll up his sleeves and sit down, and I would roll up my sleeves and sit down, never taking my eyes off him, never blinking. And he'd whip me. He had the good sense to die before I became strong enough to return the favor.

You want this gun. You beat me and it is yours. Challenge me.

LEIGH: To arm-wrestle?

BIERCE: Yes.

LEIGH: I can't arm-wrestle.

BIERCE: You have my permission to shoot me if you have to. Let's wrestle.

(*They remove their jackets.*)

HEARST: My money's on the old man.

PANCHO VILLA: *Sí. Un hombre con huevos grandes.*

(BIERCE *wins the contest.*)

BIERCE: Why did you give up?

LEIGH: I didn't give up.

BIERCE: I intend to challenge now, and be challenged in return. Christ almighty, boy, I've never been challenged in my life. I'll destroy them.

LEIGH: What do you want from me?

BIERCE: I want to know that a man who has fought for integrity and righteousness all his life in total oblivion is not leaving a son who is less prepared for the fight than he was. Take the gun. And if someone or something stops you from accomplishing the goals you believe in, shoot, boy! Shoot! Where you see corruption, shoot! Where you see immorality, shoot! Where you see—

LEIGH: Where you see what?

BIERCE: I carried a gun for thirty years and never had to fire it. Remember. The most important thing to do with this gun is display it. Prominently.

Let them know you mean business. And soon you will not need it.

LEIGH: That's how you used it.

BIERCE: That's how I used it.

PANCHO VILLA: That's not how I use it.

BIERCE: While I am away, you will work for Mr Hearst on the *Examiner*.

LEIGH: Can't I come with you? Me and Maggie?

BIERCE: You stay here and learn the business. Maggie would be of no use. I'm the People's Hope.

LEIGH: I thought nothing mattered.

BIERCE: That is what I need to know.

(*The* CHORUS *enters.*)

CHORUS #4: Ladies and gentlemen, and citizens or California, good honest people all! My friends: years from now, when your children ask you about the history of our great state, you will be able to look back to this very day. The day that the citizens of California told the Pacific Western Railroad to pack up and get the hell out of our state!

CHORUS: Hurrah!

CHORUS #4: And now...now I'm going to introduce the man whom we all turn to at this time of great crisis, the man who will put Hartford T Kent right where he belongs, the man who stands for the little people of the state, the next governor of the state of California, the honorable William Randolph Hearst!

CHORUS: Hurrah! Hurrah for Mr Hearst! He'll save the state. He'll save the country. The People's Choice!

CHORUS #2: What about the railroad?

HEARST: Ladies and gentlemen.

CHORUS #6: To war with Spain!

CHORUS #2 & CHORUS #4: To war with Spain!

CHORUS #6: We'll send you pictures!

HEARST: Not yet, not yet. I'll tell you when. Ladies and gentlemen. I congratulate you because you have chosen to take up our banner, the banner that will say to the country and to the world, "We are not going to tolerate the tyranny of the rails!"

CHORUS: Hurrah!

HEARST: I have decided to send a representative to Washington, to defeat the Funding Bill. He will, at great personal expense to me and my newspaper, stand up to Mr Hartford T Kent and refuse him his immoral, irresponsible, and unjust bill. And I pledge to you, my fellow citizens of California, that my every effort will be devoted to the deliverance of our people from the monstrous tentacles of that monopoly that threatens our very existence!

CHORUS #1: Hurrah!

HEARST: I stand as Moses stood to deliver the people from the enemies of the Lord.

CHORUS #7: Three cheers for Mr Hearst!

HEARST: That line always works.

CHORUS: Hurrah! Hurrah! Hurrah!

CHORUS #1: William Randolph Hearst for governor of California!

HEARST: You're too kind.

CHORUS #3: William Randolph Hearst for president of the United States!

HEARST: Wait a minute. Bierce, how were you planning to get to Washington? A wave of popularity?

BIERCE: On the shoulders and backs of the people, Mr Hearst. Just like you.

CHORUS #2: Scandalous!

CHORUS #4: Who does he think he is?

CHORUS #6: Yeah!

HEARST: Three cheers for Ambrose Bierce!

CHORUS #6: Three cheers for Ambrose Bierce!

HEARST: He will save the state from the tyranny of the railroad!

CHORUS: He will save the state from the tyranny of the railroad!

HEARST: With my help, of course.

CHORUS: At great personal expense to Mr Hearst.

HEARST: Now, off to Washington!

CHORUS: On the backs of the people?

HEARST: Damn right.

BIERCE: I must admit, I like the idea.

*(The CHORUS lifts BIERCE. They cross the country.)*

CHORUS #1: First stop, Nevada Territory!

CHORUS: Ambrose Bierce, the People's Hope!

BIERCE: Birth: the first and direst of all disasters.

CHORUS #2: Next stop, Colorado!

CHORUS: Colorado! Ambrose the giant killer!

BIERCE: Life: a spiritual pickle preserving the body from decay.

CHORUS #3: Nebraska, Nebraska, passing through Nebraska.

CHORUS #4: Next stop, Ioway!

CHORUS: Next stop, Ioway!

BIERCE: Cabbage: an ordinary vegetable about as large and wise as a man's head.

CHORUS #5: Let's move on to Illinois! Chicago!

BIERCE: Saint: a dead sinner, revised and edited.

*(As CHORUS members say their pieces, they abandon the crusade.)*

CHORUS #6: Next stop, Indiana: South Bend, Indianapolis, Gary!

CHORUS: Welcome to Indiana!

BIERCE: Railroad: a mechanical device enabling us to get from where we are to where we are no better off.

CHORUS #7: Ohio! Next stop Ohio!

CHORUS: Ohio!

BIERCE: I have nothing to say about Ohio.

CHORUS #8: Pennsylvania! Next stop is Pennsylvania!

CHORUS: Hurrah for Pennsylvania!

BIERCE: Adam's Apple: a lump in the throat of man to keep the rope in place.

CHORUS #8: Maryland! And Washington! Welcome to Washington, last stop.

BIERCE: Congress: a body of men who meet to repeal laws.

CHORUS #8: So here you are in Washington, D C, the Nation's Capitol. Now make a name for yourself. *(Exits)*

*(*CHORUS #4 *enters.)*

CHORUS #4: Welcome to Washington, Mr Bierce. Come by train?

BIERCE: No. I rode a moral crusade that swept me into town. Just barely.

CHORUS #4: Oh, you'll take the town by storm, no doubt. I can guarantee you that.

BIERCE: Where there is life, there is doubt. Do I know your name, sir?

CHORUS #4: Senator Harris, from the great state of Maryland. Not too far north, not too far south. And I want you to know that any friend of Mr Kent's—

BIERCE: Why do you think I am a friend of his?

CHORUS #4: You're from California, he's from California. We're impressed.

BIERCE: We?

CHORUS #4: We were guests of his, other senators and myself. Except Merton, who paid his own way.

BIERCE: Roger Merton, the poetry senator?

CHORUS #4: A good senator, but a bad poet.

BIERCE: But I look forward to meeting him.

CHORUS #4: How about at Emily's Independence Day reception?

*(A party begins forming.)*

CHORUS #4: Emily Wilton. Half the Senate's supposed to be there. Roosevelt, literary people like yourself. She asked me to invite you.

*(*MERTON *enters.)*

CHORUS #4: Here's Roger. Senator, this is Mr Bierce, the Hearst person.

MERTON: Oh yes, Bierce the writer.

BIERCE: You are an Ohioan, from Dayton? Not far from where I was born. Good.

MERTON: You seem to know me.

BIERCE: We are allies, are we not? You are chairing the hearings tomorrow and plan to help me.

MERTON: I plan to see a just and fair resolution.

BIERCE: What doubt is there that Kent is a thief, a cheat and a scoundrel?

MERTON: Mr Bierce, I intend to see a fair and just hearing, and serve the country, not to sell newspapers.

BIERCE: I am not a street hawker, Senator. I am a journalist. I write what I believe and what I believe is true. And I can vow to you that that is not the way to sell newspapers.

CHORUS #4: Oh, here's Mrs Wilton. May I present Mr Ambrose Bierce, from San Francisco.

WILTON: Oh yes. We've read your material in Bill's paper. You'll find Washington very different from San Francisco, Mr Bierce. The only hill is Capitol Hill, the only fog is Foggy Bottom, and the only man with an ounce of wit is Vice-president Roosevelt.

BIERCE: The vice-presidency, Mrs Wilton, is like the last cookie on a plate. No one wants it, but someone usually takes it.

*(Two women approach* BIERCE.*)*

CHORUS #6: Excuse me. Aren't you the writer?

BIERCE: I am a writer. History will prove if I am the writer.

CHORUS #6: Alice, I found him, Alice.

CHORUS #5: I read everything you write, sir. *Huckleberry Finn, Tom Sawyer.*

WILTON: I'm afraid you're mistaken.

CHORUS #8: Oh.

WILTON: He's not Mark Twain.

BIERCE: And *Tom Sawyer* is not a novel. It's a short story. Padded. One doesn't read a Twain book. One suffers it. A compilation of slang humor. Where are the enlightened souls who prefer wit to humor, English to slang?

*(*TWAIN *enters, arm in arm with* KENT.*)*

TWAIN: I write 'em, you read 'em. *(To* KENT*)* And then I told him, "If you carry it in your back pocket, you won't lose it." Hi, everybody!

CHORUS #4: Good evening, Mr Clemens.

TWAIN: *(To* BIERCE*)* Sam Clemens.

BIERCE: Ambrose Bierce.

TWAIN: Bierce. Bierce. Do I know you?

KENT: Mr Bierce works for Billy Hearst.

TWAIN: That's okay. We don't believe in guilt by association.

KENT: The man's sharp. He'll cut you to ribbons, Sam. Guess you didn't know Sam was here a minute ago.

BIERCE: It was too much to hope for.

WILTON: What brings you to Washington, Mr Bierce?

BIERCE: Crime, idiocy, corruption and evil incarnate. And my publisher, Mr Hearst.

KENT: You don't sound like a McKinley man.

BIERCE: I am not speaking of the President, although somebody could do the country a service by shooting him.

TWAIN: Shooting him, Bierce? I figure you could drive him out of office by just showing up and exchanging pleasantries.

KENT: Or he could bring Hearst along and browbeat him to death.

TWAIN: I got the better brows. Only use them when I have to.

*(The* CHORUS *laughs.)*

BIERCE: I was speaking of Hartford T Kent, the most wicked jackal of a robber baron that ever lived.

WILTON: Mr Bierce!

BIERCE: His tongue should be cut out and nailed to his forehead, and his head should be hoisted on a lance at the entrance to the state of California as a warning to all scoundrels that we mean business.

TWAIN: I'd resent those innuendoes, Hartford.

BIERCE: Hartford T Kent? I would like to apologize for not addressing you directly, as a villain, a robber baron and a jackal, not necessarily in that order.

WILTON: Mr Bierce!

KENT: Mr Bierce, have I done you any harm?

BIERCE: I demand satisfaction, Mr Kent. For the people you have cheated, the lives you have taken, the seventy-five million dollars you owe the government, and the service I have encountered on your railroad.

CHORUS #6: He's crazy.

CHORUS #8: He's out of his mind.

TWAIN: He's a journalist, Hartford. Says it today, writes it tonight, it's forgotten tomorrow.

BIERCE: There are worse things to be than a journalist, Mr Clemens. Best loved American humorist is one of them.

TWAIN: I'd be careful if I were you, Mr Bierce.

BIERCE: Certainly you would. Be careful! Better to be right! One tired old hack defending another. You and Kent represent what is weak, wrong, depleted and decadent about this country, this city, this party.

WILTON: Mr Bierce.

TWAIN: You're no spring chicken, Mr Bierce.

BIERCE: Neither am I a senile hypocrite, Mr Twain.

TWAIN: Them's fighting words!

(TWAIN *takes a poke at* BIERCE. *They struggle and others pull them apart.*)

CHORUS #1: Extra! Extra! Read all about it!

CHORUS #2: West Coast journalist creates near riot at party given by socialite!

CHORUS #3: Uninvited guest gives shocking display at Georgetown reception!

CHORUS #6: Best-loved humorist struck on the head by Andrew Breece!

CHORUS #5: Read all about it. Ambrose Bierce takes on the railroad!

(*All exit.*)

(*San Francisco:* HEARST *enters with a sparkler, trying to light it.* LEIGH *and* MAGGIE *follow.*)

HEARST: And everything else in the city! Happy birthday, U S of A! *Examiner* sponsors picnic and fireworks in Golden Gate Park! Free amusements and prizes! Come early!

LEIGH: Ever been on a ferris wheel before?

MAGGIE: No, never.

LEIGH: It's good for circulation, yours and the paper's. It was my idea. Billy was against it, but I pushed and he came around.

HEARST: Just the person I wanted to see. Hello, Maggie. Ready for the three-legged race?

MAGGIE: Mr Hearst, I don't want to be in no three-legged race.

HEARST: That's what you say at the end, when you're all tangled with your partner on the ground. I didn't want to do this. But you did. Having a good time?

(HEARST *grabs her around the waist, pushes* LEIGH *out of the way, as a photographer takes their picture.*)

CHORUS #1: Hold it! Got it!

HEARST: That's history! That's terrific. Make sure the little lady gets a copy, a free souvenir from the *Examiner*.

MAGGIE: Thank you, Mr Hearst.

HEARST: You're going to help me with the fireworks, aren't you, Maggie?

LEIGH: No.

MAGGIE: Sure.

HEARST: The whole kit and kaboodle'll go up faster than you can say Hearst for Governor.

MAGGIE: Hearst for Governor!

HEARST: That fast. Used to be a shot heard round the world. Now we do it civilized. *(To* LEIGH*)* Get the girl involved, boy.

LEIGH: We don't want to be in no three-legged race.

MAGGIE: C'mon, let's try. I run pretty good. *(Exits)*

LEIGH: Maggie! Maggie! *(Exits)*

HEARST: Bierce!

BIERCE: Yes, Mr Hearst?

HEARST: What's happening in Washington? Why are you causing trouble at parties? What do you know about the Funding Bill?

BIERCE: I am researching the funding of the railroad, their profits that have been hidden away, land grant bonds that were devalued—

HEARST: Facts don't sell newspapers, Bierce. Good stories do. This Merton guy who's chairing the hearings.

BIERCE: A good Senator, but a bad poet.

HEARST: He's an ally. Rewrite his poetry. Play him up. Don't argue with the man. He's running the show, readers want to hear about him. Roger Merton: writes poems, thinks great thoughts, fights hard for truth and justice. And apologize to that Mrs Wilton. She's a friend of the family, all that.

BIERCE: Mr Hearst, do you wish me to investigate the finances of the Pacific Western Railroad or mend fences better left broken?

HEARST: I want it all, Bierce. *(Exits)*

PANCHO VILLA: Señor, you are wasting your time in this country. In Mexico, if a man don't agree with me, I shoot him.

*(MERTON enters.)*

BIERCE: Senator Merton, my publisher informs me you are an honorable man. When can we fry Kent?

MERTON: Mr Bierce, I want to hear what everyone has to say. Maybe my opinions will change.

BIERCE: Man, you see black and you see white. How can you say that one is the other?

MERTON: I don't see it as black and white, Mr Bierce.

BIERCE: You should.

MERTON: Perhaps I will.

BIERCE: And when you make your decision, cut them down, Senator.

MERTON: I hope to do that.

BIERCE: Good.

MERTON: And you think that will be the Hearst side?

BIERCE: Hearst being on the right side of the issue was a mere accident, a freak of nature, a fifty-fifty chance even he was able to guess. His interest is selling newspapers. And mine is justice.

MERTON: Mr Bierce, it will be difficult to serve any cause with the kind of—if you persist—when you arrived—

BIERCE: At the party, Senator? Of the few innocent pleasures left to man over sixty, the ramming of common sense down the throats of fools is perhaps the keenest.

MERTON: Dr Johnson said that.

BIERCE: I was quoting him.

MERTON: This is a diplomatic town, Mr Bierce, where people don't necessarily say what they think.

BIERCE: Or even believe what they think?

MERTON: No. But between you and me, I was dying to say the same things, at least half of them, anyway.

BIERCE: Then you should have. Which half?

MERTON: Either half, probably.

BIERCE: Good for you.

MERTON: Everything except one comment you made about the President, Mr Bierce. As a United States senator, I find the remark repugnant. I realize it was spoken in haste.

BIERCE: It was spoken in haste because I was afraid someone would cut me off before I finished. But you think it an inopportune thing to say.

MERTON: It could be considered treason. And we could hardly expect it to help defeat the bill.

BIERCE: We stand to lose more if we vacillate in our positions, Senator. Mine are well known, unalterable, well conceived, and correct. Always. What time is the hearing tomorrow?

MERTON: Ten. I admire your candor, but I don't know how long you'll last in Washington.

BIERCE: Nothing matters.

*(They exit.)*

*(KENT enters with CHORUS as reporters.)*

KENT: Good morning, gentlemen of the press.

CHORUS: Good morning, Mr Kent.

KENT: Any questions, gentlemen?

CHORUS #1: Sir, I've heard that the railroad made over ten million dollars last year. Is that true?

KENT: I'm glad you brought that up, because that's a rumor I'd like to spike—heh-heh—get it boys?

CHORUS: Yes, sir, spike. Heh-heh.

KENT: The rumor, I can honestly say, is an unfounded one. I doubt we made one-tenth that much. No, boys, that's a story perpetrated by persons antagonistic to the progress of the railroad.

CHORUS #7: And to the nation?

KENT: And to the nation. Thank you, thank you!

CHORUS #5: Sir, we understand that there are persons, perhaps those same persons, who are organizing a lobby to fight—

KENT: Not persons, sir! Not persons, but interests! Interests that mean to further the cause of some unscrupulous individuals who mean to find personal fame and gain in my destruction.

CHORUS #4: And the railroad's?

KENT: And the railroad's!

CHORUS #7: And the nation's?

KENT: And the nation's! Thank you, thank you!

CHORUS #1: Mr Kent, Mr Kent...

KENT: Yes, sir.

CHORUS #1: Mr Kent, there's a story going around about a party last night where someone impugned—

KENT: Gentlemen, gentlemen, I know the story to which you allude. The person to whom you refer, I'm afraid, was quite— well, let's say that what he drank didn't agree with him. Heh-heh.

CHORUS: Heh-heh.

KENT: No harm to me.

CHORUS #4: Or the railroad?

KENT: Or the railroad!

CHORUS #7: Or the nation?

KENT: Or the nation! Thank you, thank you!

CHORUS: Mr Kent...Mr Kent...one more, please, look this way, Mr Kent.

KENT: Excuse me, gentlemen, excuse me, please. Ladies and gentlemen, I must beg your pardon.

(MERTON *enters. The hearing convenes.*)

MERTON: This Senate hearing into the proposed Pacific Western Railroad Funding Bill will please come to order. I would like to call Mr Hartford T Kent to the front of the chamber. W. Hartford T Kent, president of the Pacific Western Railroad?

(HEARST, MAGGIE *and* LEIGH *enter.*)

MAGGIE: Dear Mr Hearst: what is being done about the railroad?

HEARST: What've we got?

LEIGH: Merton's chairman; Wilton gives parties.

HEARST: No color?

LEIGH: "Senator Merton's literary ventures prove the impossibility of one man having two careers. Tomorrow's hearing will prove if a man can have one."

HEARST: That's not what we want on Merton. I thought Bierce could do fiction. Extra! Extra!

CHORUS #5: Railroad president to face stiff questions by Ohio committee chairman!

HEARST: Yeah, that's better.

CHORUS #3: Will Hartford Kent wither under close scrutiny?

HEARST: He better. Answer on page nine.

CHORUS #5: Read all about it on page nine!

HEARST: Now that Bierce's got their attention, we'll write Merton a letter. On the front page.

CHORUS #3: Extra! Extra! William Randolph Hearst's open letter to Funding Bill Chairman!

HEARST: Read all about it. Dear Roger: Knowing you as I do to be a steadfast and sensitive man of— you can fill the rest in yourself.

CHORUS #3: Yes, sir! *Examiner* publisher says we couldn't have asked for a better chairman!

HEARST: I did? I will!

MAGGIE: Mr Hearst, thank God for you and Mr Bierce.

HEARST: God bless you, ma'am, and thank you.

*(San Francisco faction exits.)*

*(The hearing begins.)*

MERTON: Now Mr Kent, you wish to testify on behalf of your railroad?

KENT: I do, Senator.

*(Mrs WILTON enters. She sees BIERCE.)*

WILTON: Good day, Mr Bierce.

BIERCE: I have nothing to apologize for, Mrs Wilton.

WILTON: Yes, it is a lovely day, isn't it?

KENT: Running a railroad is no bed of roses, I can assure you.

CHORUS: He's right...that's right.

BIERCE: Pleasant conversation escapes me at the moment, Mrs Wilton. I am on my way to the hearing.

WILTON: Don't make me force you into pleasantries, Mr Bierce.

BIERCE: Why do you tolerate that Kent?

WILTON: He is my friend, Mr Bierce.

KENT: Why, I don't have enough money on my person to ride my own railroad back to California!

CHORUS: Hah-hah.

BIERCE: A man is known by the company he owns, Mrs Wilton. And the company he owns has a history of fraud, deceit and immorality. And the scientist who will tell us how to recognize such a man before he acts and persuade us to kill him first will be the greatest benefactor of his century.

KENT: And if it's good enough for the English, why not the Americans?

CHORUS: He's right there, too.

MERTON: Order, please, or I shall have to clear the hearing room.

WILTON: Mr Bierce, you have quite a philosophy.

BIERCE: Purely hypothetical, Mrs Wilton.

WILTON: I would hope it remained hypothetical, Mr Bierce.

BIERCE: It has so far, Mrs Wilton.

WILTON: Good. You'd better go on. I wouldn't want you to miss an opportunity to do justice, Mr Bierce.

*(They enter the hearing room.)*

BIERCE: I shall not, Mrs Wilton.

KENT: ...nothing could be further from the truth.

MERTON: Now, Mr Kent, you stated that the cost of constructing the Pacific Western Railroad was approximately one hundred and twenty two million dollars. Do you have any statements with you to verify that?

KENT: I do, Senator.

BIERCE: The man is lying!

CHORUS #4: Senator, I object to this interruption.

MERTON: Mr Bierce, I'll have to ask you to wait your turn.

BIERCE: Has this man taken his hands out of other people's pockets long enough to be sworn in?

MERTON: Mr Bierce, would you kindly have a seat?

BIERCE: Is he under oath?

CHORUS #4: Senator!

MERTON: Everyone who testifies is under oath, Mr Bierce.

BIERCE: Then he is sworn to tell the truth. Go on.

MERTON: I'm sorry, Mr Kent.

KENT: I understand.

MERTON: Mr Kent, you may continue.

KENT: Certainly. Where was I?

CHORUS #4: At "nothing could be further from the truth."

BIERCE: Unlikely!

MERTON: Mr Bierce!

KENT: Nothing could be further from the truth...nothing could be further from...the truth. Ah, yes: nothing could be further from the truth. Without the Pacific Western Railroad, where would the farmers of California be?

BIERCE: They would be alive, Senator! I have testimony from three—

MERTON: Mr Bierce!

BIERCE: Senator, these are the facts!

CHORUS #4: Senator.

MERTON: Mr Bierce, do you wish to be removed from the hearing room?

CHORUS #4: Senator, I think this committee owes Mr Kent an apology.

MERTON: Go on, Mr Kent.

KENT: Thank you. As the railroad grows, the farmers grow. Government must allow the rails and wheat to flourish together. Would you take a little stalk of wheat, still tender before it has flowered, and pointlessly, thoughtlessly and willfully strike it down?

BIERCE: Senator, the analogy is false!

KENT: Senator Merton!

MERTON: Mr Bierce, if you don't let Mr Kent finish reading his statement, perhaps I shall have to do it myself.

BIERCE: I object to this man—

MERTON: Mr Bierce! I will have order in this hearing room. Mr Kent, may I have your statement, please?

KENT: I'm almost finished. *(He hands the paper to* MERTON.*)*

MERTON: For the record: yet there are those who would strike down our company. There are those who blame the road, and me personally, for modern society's ills, for dissatisfied farmers, socialists and anarchists who threaten our system, and even worse. It isn't the railroad, or me, personally, but conditions. Conditions, not people, are bad. And conditions, not railroads, are to blame.

BIERCE: I have no quarrel with abstractions. So far as I know, they make good citizens.

MERTON: Thank you, Mr Kent.

KENT: I wanted to set the record straight.

MERTON: Thank you, Mr Kent. You may step down.

BIERCE: Senator, I would like to address the committee.

CHORUS #1: Excuse me, Senator, this message just arrived.

MERTON: *(Reading the message)* We stand in recess until tomorrow morning.

CHORUS #4: Let's get a drink.

BIERCE: Senator Merton!

KENT: I'll buy.

BIERCE: Senator, I was scheduled to address the committee.

CHORUS #4: Roger, is this your star witness?

KENT: Bierce, wouldn't you care for a little nip?

BIERCE: Senator!

KENT: The cap's always off the bottle, Bierce.

*(KENT and CHORUS exit.)*

MERTON: Mr Bierce, the schedules of this committee are at the convenience of the United States Senate and the American public, not the deadlines of the Hearst syndicate.

BIERCE: I speak for the public. I can prove this man means to deceive this committee. But how can I do that if I am not permitted to speak?

MERTON: Are you asking me a question, Mr Bierce?

BIERCE: I want to know the answer!

MERTON: Because now is not the time! Excuse me. *(Exits)*

WILTON: I'm sorry, Mr Bierce.

BIERCE: Sorry about what, Mrs Wilton? The jackals and the Philistines are upon us.

WILTON: Upon you, Mr Bierce. *(Exits)*

PANCHO VILLA: You come visit me, amigo. We talk.

BIERCE: Dear Leigh: today they walked out on me, son. I trust you do not mind a father who is sometimes a fool.

MAGGIE: Dear Mr Bierce: I hope you are doing good in the Capitol.

BIERCE: I am doing good. I am not doing well.

HEARST: The hell you are. This isn't selling newspapers, Bierce. Oh, what did Merton think about the shooting?

BIERCE: What shooting?

CHORUS #5: Extra! Extra! Read all about it!

HEARST: McKinley got shot in Buffalo. Some anarchist.

CHORUS #5: All nation mourns our beloved president!

BIERCE: He postponed the hearings. He didn't tell me.

CHORUS #3: Mr Roosevelt takes oath at family home. Read all about it!

HEARST: Reporter's always the last to know. Get an opinion. Damn! The nomination is up for grabs!

BIERCE: My opinion is that we are better off without him.

HEARST: Bierce.

BIERCE: He was a tired old man who could have stopped the railroad. Who could have given us the moral leadership we need. Who could have—God damn me that I have anything to do with mankind! God damn yourself for dreaming up a mankind. To whom do you answer? Who judges you?

PANCHO VILLA: He's a bad man. *Hombracho.*

HEARST: I can't use this stuff, Bierce.

BIERCE: To whom am I addressed? I speak to no one. I speak for no one. I am addressed to myself. None will lead, none will follow.

PANCHO VILLA: But, Señor, nothing matters.

BIERCE: This matters. This matters.

HEARST: Bierce takes on the railroad. Takes on the President. Takes on the best loved American humorist, takes on me, high society that speaks well and common folk that can't. They were doing the Cakewalk and the Turkey Trot. He was doing a moral crusade. It's a play of the times. Ambrose Bierce takes on just about everything he runs across except the damn railroad. You go take a break. I'll have a talk with him.

*(Lights)*

END OF ACT ONE

# ACT TWO

(CHORUS, PANCHO VILLA *and* KENT *are reading papers.* BIERCE *sits typing.*)

PANCHO VILLA: Yanqui president shot in the belly. Read all about it.

CHORUS #1: Extra! Extra! All the nation mourns our beloved president!

CHORUS #2: Read all about dissatisfied anarchist who shot President McKinley!

CHORUS #3: President Roosevelt proclaims period of official mourning!

CHORUS #5: Americans gather at the Capitol to honor a great leader! Read all about it!

KENT: It was said of President Lincoln that a great tree is best measured when it is down. Mr McKinley was a man of vision who saw the greatness of America.

BIERCE: Embalm: to cure the human bacon.

KENT: And now he is lost, the victim of a deranged mind, a man who believed not in the ballot box but the bullet.

BIERCE: Idiot: a member of a large and powerful tribe whose influence in human affairs has always been dominant and controlling.

KENT: But we must remember that his legacy does not die with him. His purpose and vision must guide us in a new century.

BIERCE: In life Mr McKinley was always known for his composed manner. He is not quite decomposed.

PANCHO VILLA: I like that, amigo.

HEARST: *(Entering)* Bierce, you can't write that for a family newspaper.

BIERCE: Nothing matters. McKinley does not matter, Kent does not matter. Bierce does not matter.

HEARST: You'd better matter. Worry about the Funding Bill. This McKinley thing's pushed us off the front page. Everybody wants to read about the president. But when he's cold, I want us to be hot. One man alone may be a swell moral crusade, but Kent's got the votes. And don't tell me that that doesn't matter. *(Exits)*

BIERCE: *(Typing)* Dear Señor Villa.

PANCHO VILLA: I don't read so good the English.

BIERCE: I expect to be in Mexico soon. *Espero estar en Mexico muy pronto.*

PANCHO VILLA: *Muy bien.*

CHORUS #4: *(Entering)* Mr Bierce?

BIERCE: Senator?

CHORUS #4: Harris. From Maryland. Mr Bierce, there's someone to see you.

(ROOSEVELT *enters.*)

CHORUS #4: Mr President, this is Ambrose—

ROOSEVELT: Bierce, I'm Roosevelt. Don't get up. Harris, don't sit down.

CHORUS #4: Yes, sir.

ROOSEVELT: Wait outside.

CHORUS #4: Yes, sir.

ROOSEVELT: Out of earshot.

CHORUS #4: Yes, sir.

ROOSEVELT: That's good. That's very good.

(CHORUS #4 *exits.*)

ROOSEVELT: He'll listen at the keyhole. No matter. What are you writing?

BIERCE: Cobwebs, from an empty skull.

ROOSEVELT: I'm a writer myself. What do you think of Twain?

BIERCE: Nothing.

ROOSEVELT: Enough chat. I didn't come here to talk about books. I've been watching this railroad thing. Maybe they want to get the oil, steamships, the automobile and who knows what else and run American transportation, one big company, with all the ends, means and roadways in the country under their power. Maybe they don't. It's not my concern right now; it's yours. But I don't want them destroying this beautiful land we've got, and it is a beautiful land. I can't give you active support.

BIERCE: I am aware of it.

ROOSEVELT: You are not. Don't interrupt. You're worse than the miscreant who hired you. This is your fight and it's a good fight.

BIERCE: If the railroad is defeated, the land will be protected.

ROOSEVELT: Let's make sure the land is protected.

BIERCE: If the railroad is defeated, the land will be protected.

ROOSEVELT: I heard you the first time. Let's make sure the land is protected. This senator, outside...

BIERCE: Senator not-too-far-north-not-too-far-south?

ROOSEVELT: That's the one. He's quite a friend of the railroad man.

BIERCE: I have observed, Mr President, that friendship is the kind of ship that is big enough in fair weather for two. In foul weather, it's only big enough for one.

ROOSEVELT: That's good. That's damn good. I don't trust him, Bierce. That's why I brought him along. You know this visit is off the record; it never happened.

BIERCE: If you wish. I will say nothing.

ROOSEVELT: He will. Rumors travel fast in this town, and it couldn't hurt your cause. I'll wish you luck, Bierce. Do you believe in luck?

BIERCE: I believe in right.

ROOSEVELT: Right! The right to live, the right to fight—

BIERCE: The right to have measles and the like.

ROOSEVELT: Yes. Don't get up. Want some advice, Bierce?

BIERCE: Do you, sir?

ROOSEVELT: We understand each other. Good day. *(Exits)*

CHORUS #4: *(Entering)* Well, Mr Bierce, that was quite an honor.

BIERCE: Indeed it was, Senator. Indeed it was. The President must think highly of you to have you arrange this meeting.

CHORUS #4: It was nothing.

BIERCE: You're wrong, Senator. It mattered greatly.

CHORUS #4: I'm happy to help out.

BIERCE: And you did, Senator. You did.

CHORUS #4: There's more to running a railroad than laying track and stoking engines, Mr Bierce.

BIERCE: I'm sure you know more than that, Senator.

CHORUS #4: What I know is not common knowledge, Mr Bierce.

BIERCE: Perhaps it ought to be common, Senator.

CHORUS #4: Perhaps we can keep our lines of communication open, Mr Bierce.

BIERCE: An excellent suggestion, Senator. Good day.

(CHORUS #4 *exits.*)

BIERCE: Copy!

(CHORUS #5 *takes copy to* HEARST.)

HEARST: Bierce, this stuff looks good, looks good. Now let's make it sound good.

CHORUS #5: Extra! Extra! *Examiner* uncovers evidence of corporate deceit!

HEARST: I like that! Corporate deceit.

CHORUS #5: Bierce vows: Mr Kent on the grill; will toast to a nut brown.

HEARST: He did? He will!

(KENT, MERTON *and* CHORUS *gather for hearing.*)

BIERCE: Mr Kent is not altogether bad. Though severe, he is merciful. He says ugly things of his enemy, but has the decency to be careful that they are mostly lies.

MERTON: Mr Kent, do you swear to tell the truth, the whole truth, and nothing but the truth, so help you God?

KENT: I do.

MERTON: Mr Kent, you've sworn that the reason your railroad is asking the Senate to refund payments is—

KENT: Is for the purpose of making improvements.

(*As* BIERCE *types,* CHORUS *members pull the sheets from his typewriter and read his copy.*)

MERTON: I see. Specifically for what, Mr Kent?

KENT: For improvements.

CHORUS #6: Truthful: dumb and illiterate.

MERTON: I understand that, Mr Kent. What we'd like to know is, what sort of improvements did you have in mind?

KENT: To make the trains run better.

MERTON: And how do you propose to do that, Mr Kent?

KENT: By making improvements.

(CHORUS #2 *whispers in* KENT's *ear and hands him a piece of paper.*)

CHORUS #7: Responsibility: a detachable burden easily shifted to the shoulders of God or one's neighbor.

MERTON: Mr Kent, I'm afraid you don't understand. Before the Senate can consider your request, we must have some facts.

KENT: Senator Merton, I would like to answer you with a statement which I have just this moment received.

MERTON: Go ahead, Mr Kent.

KENT: Thank you. The Pacific Western Railroad has been instrumental in guaranteeing the economic stabilization of the great state of California and its brother and sister states and territories by the provision of transportation for the profit and comfort and health and security of all people. Built in 1876—

(CHORUS #2 *whispers in his ear.*)

CHORUS #8: Positive: mistaken at the top of one's voice.

KENT: —Built in 1867 at a cost of nearly eighty-seven million dollars, the result of private enterprise...

MERTON: Excuse me once again, Mr Kent.

KENT: I'm not finished reading my statement.

MERTON: Mr Kent, you stated—or you read—that it cost eighty-seven million dollars to build your railroad.

KENT: Let me find my place. Yes, I did.

CHORUS #6: Fib: a lie that has not cut its teeth.

MERTON: In our last session you swore that the cost of construction was one hundred twenty-two million dollars.

KENT: I did.

MERTON: Then how do you explain the fact that you just said it cost eighty-seven million dollars to build?

KENT: That's what it cost.

MERTON: Then why didn't you say eighty-seven million dollars in the first place? Why one hundred twenty-two million dollars?

KENT: Because I thought it was one hundred twenty-two million dollars.

CHORUS #1: Kleptomaniac: a rich thief.

MERTON: And today you think it cost eighty-seven million dollars?

KENT: I believe so.

MERTON: You believe so? But why did you quote a different figure the other day?

KENT: I was mistaken, but only by thirty or forty million dollars.

MERTON: Do you mean to stand there and tell me that you could be that wrong about the cost of building the railroad of which you are president and co-founder?

(CHORUS #2 *whispers into* KENT'*s ear.*)

KENT: I'm afraid I just wasn't sure, Senator. How am I supposed to know these things?

MERTON: If you don't know how much money it cost you to start your own business, who would?

KENT: My bookkeepers.

MERTON: Then perhaps you should ask your bookkeepers to come in here tomorrow, so you can be more sure of yourself. What do you think?

KENT: Of course, Senator, I think that—

(CHORUS #2 *whispers into his ear.*)

KENT: Is that all, Senator?

MERTON: Yes, Mr Kent, that will be all for today. You may step down.

CHORUS #3: Reporter: a writer who guesses his way to the truth and dispels it with a tempest of words.

MERTON: Mr Bierce? Do you wish to testify?

BIERCE: Thank you. Senator, I would like to make only one observation. Mr Kent was misinformed when he stated—or swore—that it cost him and his fellow villains $87,000,000. The fact is, Senator, that construction of the Pacific Western Railroad was accomplished for the sum of $56,240,000 and some change.

(*The* CHORUS *murmers.*)

MERTON: Mr Bierce, can you prove that statement?

BIERCE: I can.

CHORUS #2: Senator, this is all very interesting, but what does it have to do with whether or not the Pacific Western gets the loan deferment?

BIERCE: What does it have to do? Here is a man who has stood up in a hearing chamber of the Senate of the United States of America and sworn to tell the truth, only to find out that he hasn't the slightest idea of what the truth is! This man confesses that he has no knowledge of the workings of his own company, and you think that he should be given seventy-five million dollars? This man has cheated, bribed legislators, and lied through his teeth every time he wore them. He deserves to hang from every branch of every tree in every state and territory penetrated by his railroad, with the exception of Nevada, which has no trees. Yet this notorious old man can stand here before a committee of the highest legislative body of his country and make an oath that he is an honest and unselfish man. I am surprised he is even allowed to show his face in public.

CHORUS #1: He's right!

(KENT *exits.*)

BIERCE: That is all I have to say.

CHORUS #1 & CHORUS #7: Mr Bierce! Mr Bierce! Senator Merton!

CHORUS #5: Extra! Extra! Hartford Kent contradicts himself on stand!
He admits he knows nothing of corporate finance!

CHORUS #6: Extra! Extra! Senator Merton's committee catches Mr Kent in a
great error! Read all about it in the *Examiner!*

CHORUS #8: Hartford Kent contradicted by reporter for the Hearst papers!

HEARST: That's telling them!

WILTON: I'm sure you thanked him.

MERTON: Thanked him! I can't even talk to him. I show him my poetry;
he returns it without a word.

WILTON: That's not how to approach the man, Roger.

MERTON: The man is unapproachable.

WILTON: You must be tactful.

MERTON: How long have you had this secret, Emily?

WILTON: It's no secret. We met in the park the other evening. I was walking
along, and I looked out on the pond, and there he was, in a little rowboat.
Ahoy, there, Mr Bierce, taking chances with our Washington nights, I see.

BIERCE: Yes, madam, but only at sea. Washington has not had a case of
piracy in over a hundred and twenty years. I looked it up.

WILTON: How very cautious of you, Mr Bierce.

BIERCE: Thorough, Mrs. Wilton.

WILTON: Do you come here looking for pirates very often, Mr Bierce?

BIERCE: Only when my good friend, the Maharajah of Modesto, is out of
town. He allows me the privilege of using his yacht.

WILTON: Does he? I imagine you are a great friend of the Maharajah.

BIERCE: I am his only friend, Mrs Wilton, and he mine. Unfortunately, as he
is out of town most of the time, I am forced to make the most of it as best I
can.

WILTON: By yourself?

BIERCE: In good company, nevertheless. I am captain, navigator, deck hand,
galley slave, night watch—

WILTON: But not social director.

BIERCE: The what?

WILTON: You have no passengers, Mr Bierce. You have no one to look after.

BIERCE: No, Mrs Wilton, there are no passengers aboard this ship.

WILTON: You are your own passenger. How very much I admire you, Mr Bierce, to be all things in one. Some people are mixers, I suppose. And I'm one of them.

BIERCE: I wonder if you'd care to join me.

WILTON: Oh, that's very kind of you, Mr Bierce, but you needn't offer. I really must go.

BIERCE: Mrs Wilton, at times the demands of this craft are too great for one man. I can't—cannot be all things at the same time. The Maharajah told me I could have a guest aboard. If you are not too busy.

WILTON: The Maharajah said that?

BIERCE: The Maharajah allows for human weakness, Mrs Wilton. There is room enough for two.

WILTON: Are you certain, Mr Bierce, that your friend would consent?

BIERCE: He would approve wholeheartedly, I can assure you. In fact, he might even actively encourage you.

WILTON: In that case, Captain, I couldn't object, could I?

MERTON: And then what happened?

WILTON: Senator?

MERTON: I'm sorry. I meant...

WILTON: Senator, I made a friend. (*Exits*)

MERTON: Mr Bierce, I'm glad things are going so well. Ambrose.

BIERCE: Well, Senator?

MERTON: Yes. Well. In general. The hearings. And all. The tide is turning.

BIERCE: It was your questions, Senator. Roger, it was your questions. You had him. Mr Kent is not the moral pachyderm we have always believed him to be.

MERTON: We? You never believed him.

BIERCE: I am harder on myself, Senator.

MERTON: Moral pachyderm. I quoted you in the paper today. I didn't realize you were going to use it. The look of agony?

BIERCE: No problem.

MERTON: Nothing matters?

BIERCE: No. Nothing does matter. Except this.

(CHORUS *and* KENT *enter for the hearings.*)

CHORUS #5: Ambrose Bierce predicts hard times ahead for Hartford Kent! He outlines objections to Funding Bill!

CHORUS #1: Extra! Extra! Hartford Kent to bring books to Congress!

CHORUS #5: Which one is telling the truth? Extra! Extra! Find out today!

MERTON: Mr Kent, this committee would like to study your books. Have you brought them with you?

KENT: Senator, last night we had an accident. There was a fire in our accounting office, and in our haste to save our records, we seem to have lost them.

MERTON: You lost them?

KENT: Yes, sir.

MERTON: Mr Kent, before your unfortunate accident, did you happen to check the books and find out how much your railroad actually cost to construct?

KENT: I believe it was closer to the other figure.

MERTON: Which other figure?

KENT: The lower one.

MERTON: I can't hear you, Mr Kent.

KENT: The one in the paper. The fifty-six something.

MERTON: Could you speak up, Mr Kent?

KENT: It was fifty-six something.

BIERCE: Senator, it was $56,240,323 and some change. This man should be used as a decoy in shooting matches.

MERTON: Mr Kent, you have come to Washinton to receive a favor from your government, and yet twice you have come within an inch of perjuring yourself. Can you give me good reason why you should not be held in contempt of this committee?

KENT: Senator, I have a statement I'd like to read: the Pacific Western Railroad has always sought to—

MERTON: Mr Kent, I don't want to hear another essay on your railroad! I want to know what happened to the moral pachyderm who wandered in here and asked for seventy-five million dollars.We stand in recess.

KENT: —provide people with opportunity. Last week, two hundred and fifty Chinese laborers were given the day off, with pay.

HEARST: Page one. I want artists' renditions of the fires. Did the case of the Pacific Western go up in smoke?

CHORUS #1: Extra! Extra! No suspect in railroad fire! P W prez denies knowledge of any wrongdoing! Read all about it!

CHORUS #3: Bierce lashes out at bewildered railroad president!

HEARST: Read all about it!

KENT: Mr Bierce.

BIERCE: Yes?

KENT: Being caught with my pants down makes me thirsty. How about a drink?

BIERCE: I was going with friends and acquaintances.

KENT: I don't mind tagging along. Yep, Bierce, you undid my suspenders and dropped my shorts without even mussing my jacket. I admire that.

BIERCE: *(To* WILTON, *across stage)* I was walking along the street after the hearing and chanced to wander into the gutter. And I found our friend Kent, searching for a manhole cover to hide under. Homesick, no doubt. He offered me a bribe, Emily. One hundred thousand dollars. I told him my price was seventy-five million dollars.

WILTON: Within earshot of everyone in the vicinity, I suppose. I'm sure he was only joking with you.

KENT: Yes, I admire that in a man. You could be more than a reporter, Bierce. You could do a lot, go far.

BIERCE: The man tried to bribe me, in front of witnesses. He offered me a fortune to leave him alone. What I could do with that money!

WILTON: You could forget about your moral crusade.

BIERCE: If I wished.

WILTON: Hartford was just having some fun.

KENT: Little bourbon on troubled waters, eh, Bierce? You're worth a lot more than whatever Hearst's paying you. In the right position, money would be no problem.

BIERCE: A hundred thousand dollars?

KENT: That would be no problem.

BIERCE: *(To* WILTON*)* Joking? He was deadly serious. He has got to get rid of me! He said it himself. I said every man has his price, he said a hundred thousand dollars. I told him seventy-five million. They are using it in tomorrow's paper.

WILTON: He wasn't serious. You know the way he is.

BIERCE: The man was serious. And I do not know the way he is.

WILTON: Then how do you know he meant it? Ambrose, that story will be an embarrassment to him. And to you. Hartford Kent is no fool. He wouldn't do something like that.

BIERCE: And he tried to buy me a glass of whiskey! Bribery is bribery!

WILTON: Ambrose, I can't believe that happened. I shall be very disappointed if you print that story.

BIERCE: I file stories. Hearst prints them.

WILTON: Then don't file it. You could stop it.

BIERCE: I cannot.

WILTON: You're destroying a man, not defeating him. But will you listen? You're too convinced of your own righteousness. You're a stubborn fool!

BIERCE: I am a stubborn fool! If being right and standing by my convictions makes me a stubborn fool, then, by God, I am. If it means standing alone above the rabble, then, by God, I shall. If that makes me stubborn, if that makes me an ass, so be it. I will stand fast against your kind.

WILTON: My kind?

BIERCE: Your kind, their kind, that kind! I have no business with venality and furry sentiment!

WILTON: Then have no business with me.

HEARST: Hurrah for Ambrose Bierce!

CHORUS #3: Ambrose Bierce offered huge bribe by Hartford Kent!

HEARST: Read all about it!

MAGGIE: Extra! Extra! Read all about the man who couldn't be bought!

BIERCE: Read all about it! Hearst has his story, Roosevelt his secrecy, Twain his reputation, Kent his just reward and everyone else his distance, her distance. At a cost of neither pride nor dignity nor friendship nor principle.

HEARST: I'm glad I hired him. I'm looking better every day.

CHORUS #1: William Randolph Hearst proclaims I'm glad I hired him! In statement released today! Read all about it!

HEARST: Bierce, this is starting to look good. So good, we might want to do a little piece on you. I'll do it myself, Ambrose.

BIERCE: You may call me Bierce, Mr Hearst.

HEARST: The whole picture. Ambrose the giant-killer! Journalist, adventurer, soldier, father. Like what advice you'd give to a young writer starting out.

BIERCE: Avoid newspapers, believe nothing you see or hear, and seek the good advice of squirrels.

HEARST: Huh. That what you tell your kid?

BIERCE: Kid?

HEARST: Son. Son. Kid is a son. You raise your son, give him advice. How do you raise a son? That might be a good column.

BIERCE: I always turn to the wisdom of the Bible, Mr Hearst. The philosophers there tell me how to raise children.

HEARST: Yeah? Like who?

BIERCE: Herod.

HEARST: Ever been to Cuba? Little Spanish island with big trouble and smooth cigars. You smoke cigars? Have one. *(He tosses* BIERCE *a cigar.)*

BIERCE: Thank you. Are you offering me a job in Cuba, Mr Hearst.

HEARST: I'm offering you a cigar, and a chance to pick up a few on your own. Nationally syndicated. No telling what's going to happen in Cuba. Then maybe Panama. Or Europe. Who knows?

BIERCE: Who does know?

HEARST: You will. People are interested in the world around them. And they're interested in what you think about it.

BIERCE: Cuba.

HEARST: Soon as you finish this matter here, *vaya con Dios.*

PANCHO VILLA: *Vaya con diablo.*

HEARST: Enjoy the cigar. Smokes real nice, doesn't it?

BIERCE: Cuba! What I could do in Cuba! Leigh? Your father is going to Cuba!

*(*MAGGIE *enters as* BIERCE *lights his cigar.)*

MAGGIE: Well, what happened was, there was a disturbance at the place where I work. He—Leigh Bierce, the deceased— thought I was flirting with one of our regular customers. And no one wanted any trouble, least of all me and the customer, but Leigh had a gun he was fond of using to get his way. His evidence, he used to call it. Well, there was a struggle and there was a gun and there was some shots. And that's what happened.

CHORUS #1: Journalist's son shot dead in barroom brawl!

CHORUS #2: Son of prominent man found dead. Read all about it!

MAGGIE: Mr Bierce?

BIERCE: Who is it?

MAGGIE: It's Maggie, Mr Bierce. Matthew's Maggie.

(KENT *and* MERTON *appear on the opposite side of the stage.*)

KENT: Senator Merton, may I have a word with you?

MAGGIE: I'm sorry about your son, Mr Bierce.

BIERCE: You needn't be. He was like his father, Maggie.

MAGGIE: Then he was a good man.

BIERCE: Hot, stubborn and right. Always.

KENT: Roger, I think we should postpone the hearing for a week so Ambrose can arrange a burial.

MERTON: If he so chooses, we can arrange it.

MAGGIE: You shared my grief, Mr Bierce. I come to share yours.

BIERCE: Your husband died for a cause. I could share that, Maggie.

MAGGIE: Knowing Matthew died for a cause don't keep me warm at night, but thank you. I'm sorry this happened.

BIERCE: I was not a good father.

MAGGIE: You can't judge.

BIERCE: I do. I judge. I judge. I was not a good father.

MAGGIE: He's dead.

BIERCE: We are diminished.

MAGGIE: Mr Bierce, you should know we'll get him a box and a place to rest.

BIERCE: Thank you.

KENT: *(To* BIERCE*)* Oh. Excuse me. I didn't know you had company.

BIERCE: Maggie, this is Kent.

MAGGIE: The railroad man.

KENT: I am the railroad man.

(MAGGIE *exits.*)

KENT: A son or a daughter's death is always premature. Whatever the age, if a child is buried by its parents, it died young. I laid my oldest boy to rest two years ago. He was twenty-six. I have another son that's sixteen. Two daughters; I'm a grandfather four times. I can't give you false consolation. It's hard, but it's a lot harder six months from now, when others have forgotten and moved on with life. I wanted you to know that I know how you feel, and I can appreciate what it takes out of you as you grow older and fail to forget.

BIERCE: Yes.

KENT: I'd like to put a train at your disposal, if you'd like to be home for a few days. Or, if you prefer, I could arrange for your son to be brought here. Roger could postpone the hearings.

BIERCE: How did you manage to come here?

KENT: As a friend. I'm sorry about your loss. And the publicity.

BIERCE: Nothing there matters. But I am amazed that you have the audacity to come to me as a friend and offer a free ride to my son after you cheated and murdered that woman's husband to pay the fare.

KENT: My work in the railroad has nothing to do with this visit. Can't you see I come as one father to another?

BIERCE: No. Your deeds live with you and define you, Kent, and you may not wipe your bloody hands on Leigh's shroud or my sentiments.

*(The hearing convenes.)*

BIERCE: Senator, Mr Kent's generosity to my family serves to illustrate a point that I have been hammering away at throughout the hearings. This man is known for his lip service to nobility. He gave seven women a hundred dollars each after killing their husbands. And he offers a train for my son, who would have refused it himself and walked if he could. I told you once, sir, my price is seventy-five million dollars! The spectacle of this old man standing on the brink of eternity, his pockets loaded with dishonest gold which he knows neither how to enjoy nor to whom to bequeath, swearing it is the fruit of honest labor and beseeching an opportunity to multiply the store, is one of the most pitiable sights it has ever been my lot to observe.

CHORUS #5: Extra! Extra! Senate deadlocked on Funding Issue! Neither side willing to budge!

CHORUS #4: Roger, let's be realistic. They've paid back every creditor but the government. We can wait.

MERTON: That's not the issue, Bob!

*(ROOSEVELT enters.)*

ROOSEVELT: Gentlemen.

MERTON: Mr President.

ROOSEVELT: I'll come to the point. You can talk all day and all you'll get is that Kent is a son of a bitch and if he got what he deserved for grabbing everything he thought he deserved, he'd be in a heap of trouble. But so would we. We can't go back to covered wagons. This is what I want.

CHORUS #1: Extra! Extra! The impossible comes true! The people prevail!

HEARST: Good leadership is what it was!

CHORUS #3: Good leadership is what it was! proclaims William Randolph Hearst. He announces his candidacy. Read all about it! Senator, how do you feel about the compromise?

CHORUS #4: We feel it was the only alternative.

CHORUS #5: Are you satisfied?

MERTON: Each side gave a little. And everyone was given fair treatment, the United States government included.

CHORUS #7: Mr Kent, how do you feel about the compromise?

KENT: It could've been worse, could've been better. We got a fair hearing. I just hope I don't have to raise my fares any.

BIERCE: What about the farmers? What about the perjury? What about justice? This is no victory. This is a compromise!

PANCHO VILLA: Señor, you are wasting your time in this country. In Mexico, if a man don't agree with me, I shoot him.

HEARST: Bierce, I came to Washington special—nice town—to give you a little token of our appreciation. Three cheers for the man who couldn't be bought. Hip-hip?

PANCHO VILLA & CHORUS: Hurrah! Hurrah! Hurrah!

HEARST: Good. A little golden watch on a golden chain from the Golden State. Our state. Heh-heh. You did it, Bierce. I had a little speech but I'm running late. We got deadlines!

(HEARST *exits with* CHORUS.)

BIERCE: I thought my battle was here.

PANCHO VILLA: No, Señor.

BIERCE: So if they hear of my being stood up against a wall in Mexico and shot to rags, they should know I think it a pretty good way to depart this life.

PANCHO VILLA: Señor, I could use a watch.

(BIERCE *throws him the watch.*)

BIERCE: I think the reason you Mexican bandits wear two belts of ammunition is because you are notoriously bad shots.

PANCHO VILLA: Watch your mouth, amigo.

BIERCE: Nothing matters.

WILTON: I know you don't believe that, Ambrose.

BIERCE: I must. I must believe it. To be a gringo in Mexico. That, indeed, is euthanasia.

PANCHO VILLA: Hey, gringo! You come tell me your English lessons now, no? It is pretty good, don't you no think?

BIERCE: Señor Villa, your English is terrible. *¡Que cosa, pendejo es estupido! ¡Vamonos!*

PANCHO VILLA: I speak the best English in all of Mexico! Hey, gringo!

(BIERCE *exits.*)

HEARST: Ambrose Bierce takes on Mexico. And as far as anybody knows, he got his wish. Don't matter, one way or the other. His kind are gone. So's the railroad. And that's the way it happened. And just remember where you read it. You read it right here.

*(Lights)*

END OF PLAY

# CHOPIN IN SPACE

CHOPIN IN SPACE opened at the Yale Repertory Theater, (Lloyd Richards, Artistic Director) on 27 January 1984 as part of the Rep's Winterfest. The cast and creative contributors were:

FREDERIC CHOPIN/LECH WALESA ......................... Dann Florek
MARYA/DANUTA ........................................ Laila Robins
THE BEAR ............................................Allen Evans
THE TANKS ........................... Toni Isbell & Jonathan Emerson
STASH/HITLER/DELACROIX ............................... Bill Cohen
BEEZO/GEORGE SAND .................................. Robin Bartlett
THE POPE/F D R/RONALD REAGAN ...................... Robert Lesser
BABCI/ELEANOR ROOSEVELT ......................Christian Clemenson
A MAN WITH A HANGOVER ............................... Tom Isbell
A MAN WITH A FLOWER/HARRY TRUMAN .............. Jonathan Emerson

*Director* ...........................................James A Simpson
*Sets* ............................................. Michael Yeargan
*Lights* ................................................ Bill Warfel
*Costumes* ......................................... Candice Donnelly

CHOPIN IN SPACE was first performed in New York City on 9 May 1985 at The Ark Theater, (Bruce Daniel, Donald Marcus, and Lisa Milligan Artistic Directors). The cast and creative contributors were:

FREDERIC CHOPIN/LECH WALESA ..................... Noble Shropshire
MARYA/DANUTA .........................................Nancy Mette
THE BEAR ............................................. Paul Romero
THE TANKS ...........................Philip Lenkowsky & Rick Thomas
STASH/HITLER/DELACROIX ...........................William Mesnik
BEEZO/GEORGE SAND ..............................Mary Lou Rosato
THE POPE/F D R/RONALD REAGAN .................William Duff-Griffin
BABCI/ELEANOR ROOSEVELT .............................. Sylvia Short
A MAN WITH A HANGOVER/A MAN WITH A FLOWER ......Philip Lenkowsky
HARRY TRUMAN ......................................... Rick Thomas

*Director* ................................................ Rebecca Guy
*Scenery* ...............................................Anne Servanton
*Costumes* .......................................... Catherine Zuber
*Lights* ...............................................Bruce Daniel

The author is indebted to New Dramatists, the Midwest Playwrights Program and Humboldt State University's New Play Program for their encouragement and work in realizing the final script.

The play takes place all over the map.

# AUTHOR'S NOTES

After seeing several productions of this play, I'm convinced that simple is better than elaborate. Don't forget: it's a piano he's after, not a symphony orchestra. It's easy to overwhelm this show with tech. When MARYA and CHOPIN go to Washington to visit the ROOSEVELTS, she apologizes for their low-tech record player. She could just as easily be apologizing for the whole production style.

I've sometimes wondered how this show would be done by a bunch of kids in their backyard, with only one room of the house to use as a source of props.

ACTING. The style of the piece is basically realistic, but don't waste time wondering what these people had for breakfast. The fun of the piece is that real people find themselves in amazing situations and are forced to cope. Here's a Romantic dandy of a musician travelling through a series of events that demand a Byronic hero. Imagine his chagrin. Think Monty Python. That absolute commitment to unlikely reality.

CASTING. Actors play multiple roles that are intended to stress the similarity of the characters they play. Obviously, CHOPIN and WALESA are both heroes dear to the Polish people. HITLER, DELACROIX and STASH all make pictures, then politics. The POPE, F D R, and REAGAN are all caught somewhere between politics and performance (remember that the Pope was an actor before he was a seminarian). And, neither the BEAR nor HARPO speak.

ACCENTS. The less, the better.

BLACKOUTS. The blackouts should be like musical rests, not intermissions. They're not an excuse to move chunks of scenery around. I listened to Chopin's Preludes a lot when I was writing the play, and I loved the way the mood, length and pace of each short piece would immediately be countered by the next. Long black-outs kill the energy of the piece.

CHOPIN/LECH and MARYA/DANUTA. CHOPIN gradually becomes LECH during the play (you'll notice LECH-like political comments creeping into the pianist's speeches). In the end, of course, he realizes that he serves his country best by realizing its music. MARYA, more the pragmatist, leaps into her DANUTA character whenever Poland needs her.

BEEPS. During the second line scene, a beeping starts that continues until CHOPIN gets busted. I hear a single, steady piano note, used to help create an eerie tension. You might find other places in the show where this could be used.

Finally, if you get to the point where audiences are torn between laughing and crying, you're doing something terrifically right.

PRONUNCIATIONS AND BACKGROUND

Sto Lat (Stow Lat): Literally, "may you live a hundred years!" a traditional Polish toast.

Warszawa (Var SHA vah): the Polish name for Warsaw, capital of Poland.

Marya (MAR ey ah)

Babci (BAAB chee): grandma

Nowy Swiat (No vee SCHVEE ut): a street in Warsaw, something like Fifth Avenue.

The Black Madonna is Mary, the patroness of Poland. When Lech Walesa was awarded the Nobel Prize, he journeyed to the Shrine of the Black Madonna and placed it in the church.

Chopin's heart had a similarly romantic end, just as the play states. His body is in Paris, his heart is at the Church of the Holy Cross in Warsaw, where it is greatly revered.

*(CHOPIN alone)*

CHOPIN: Good evening. My name is Frederick Chopin. The music you hear in the background. Sound familiar? Perhaps you recognize it as one of the great popular melodies of all time. *Till the End of Time.* But not many of you may realize that *Till the End of Time* is actually the melody from my Polonaise in A Major, Opus 53, a piece of music I composed nearly one hundred and fifty years ago. Is that right? Now, through the miracle of the recording industry, this great tune and more are yours, available in this beautiful album at a popular price. You know, many people ask me: Fred, Freddie, Frederick, where did you get the idea for this piece? Did you have to think about it, or did it just come to you like in a dream? Or what?

*(Blackout)*

*(Poland. MARYA sits, CHOPIN's head in her lap. She strokes his hair idly.)*

MARYA: Chopin, I was wondering.

CHOPIN: What?

MARYA: Could you go out into the world and, you know, take simple country songs of our native homeland and turn them into something the world will love? You know. Could you make your piano sing for Poland?

*(CHOPIN sits up.)*

CHOPIN: Sure. But not here. *(He gets up to leave.)*

MARYA: Wait. Where are you going?

CHOPIN: Paris. I need perspective. But I'll be back.

MARYA: Before you go: Take this spoonful of earth as a symbol of our native homeland. So that wherever you go, there is Poland.

*(She scoops up some earth. Before she can give it to him, a BEAR comes out, grabs the earth and eats it. The BEAR exits.)*

MARYA: Don't worry. There's more. Take this spoonful of earth *(She scoops up more earth.)* as a symbol of our native homeland, so that wherever...

*(A tank enters. HITLER steps out, swipes the earth and rumbles off.)*

MARYA: In foreign lands they may reward you better, but they cannot love you more.

*(BEEZO enters.)*

BEEZO: Oh yes we can.

*(CHOPIN stumped.)*

CHOPIN: I'll be back.

*(Blackout)*

*(CHOPIN lies dead. MARYA and BEEZO address the audience.)*

MARYA: He never came back. I still wait for my Chopin.

BEEZO: The spirit of Frederick Chopin was extinguished on the morning of October 17th, in the company of his sister Louise, an artist who sketched his head, other women. And me.

MARYA: There is much sadness in Poland.

BEEZO: We set the scene: a full moon, hidden by rain clouds. Place Vendome. Paris.

MARYA: Church bells, they ring every hour for my Chopin.

BEEZO: Second floor, facing the street. Chopin's head is thrown back on a pillow, his Adam's apple prominent, eyes closed, lips partly open.

MARYA: He speaks letters to loved ones in Polish....

BEEZO: He spoke the name of a single woman in that room. His neck exposed, his blouse open to help him breathe. He dies of consumption, the death of an artist. Outside it is raining; inside he is drowning. His face is cast, his hands are cast, his picture drawn. *(She holds up the sketch.)* See, here's the sketch. *(She holds up the mask.)* And here's the mask. *(She holds up the hands.)* And here are his hands. Frederick Chopin. And he died.

MARYA: With the word Poland on his lips, drifting out in space, Poland, Poland. Never die, Chopin.

BEEZO: There is a post-mortem examination by a prominent physician. And a church service where Mozart's Requiem would be sung. All this cost money. He died without a sou.

MARYA: Will you stop!

BEEZO: You Poles never have any money. Champagne taste, beer purse. *(Holds up the hands)* The hands of an artist

MARYA: Give me those. They belong to Poland.

BEEZO: They do not. He was half French. It was very beautiful. *(She exits.)*

MARYA: The funeral was delayed because there was difficulty having women sing in a church service. And, following his request, Chopin's heart was removed from his body... *(She reaches into CHOPIN's chest and pulls out a record.)* ...and was taken to the Church of the Holy Cross in his native Warszawa, and placed there in an urn, where it beat for Poland. Where it still beats for Poland.

*(She plays the record on an old Victrola. Opus 40, #1. Polonaise in A Minor. The record plays. A* TANK *comes out.)*

MARYA: Don't worry. The music will stop the tank.

*(The* TANK *blasts the speakers. The* TANK *exits.* MARYA *turns the record with her finger, humming along.)*

MARYA: It still plays, the Polonaise!

*(A* BEAR *enters, smashes the record player, and carries* MARYA *off. Blackout)*

*(*CHOPIN *and* MARYA*, idly.)*

MARYA: Chopin, I was wondering.

CHOPIN: What?

MARYA: Could you go out into Poland and lead a rebellion against the occupying powers and unite all Poles? You know, and be my husband and live on the fourteenth floor of a cramped apartment in Gdansk? Maybe call our movement Solidarity, because shipworkers, farmers, even actors, would all be working for a chance to let Poland be Poland?

CHOPIN: Wait a minute. That wasn't the plan. The piano is my mistress.

MARYA: Let Poland be your mistress.

CHOPIN: I was on my way to Paris.

MARYA: Would you listen to the Pope? He's Polish, too. Holy Father?

*(The* POPE *enters.)*

MARYA: Can you talk to him?

POPE: As Christ our savior led His people, so, too, shall you lead Poland. As Christ our Beacon delivered His people, so shall you deliver Poland. This has been foretold.

CHOPIN: By whom? If you'll excuse me, I was on my way...somewhere.

*(*BABCI *enters.)*

BABCI: Is this the end of the line?

CHOPIN: It's not a line.

BABCI: What are we waiting for?

CHOPIN: To sing for Poland.

BABCI: I'll wait for that.

CHOPIN: Thank you. You don't have to.

BABCI: I walk all over Warszawa. This is the shortest line.

CHOPIN: What are you waiting for?

BABCI: Television.

CHOPIN: What's that?

MARYA: Why do you want a television? There's only one station left.

BABCI: I could see the Pope.

MARYA: Here is Pope. Here. You don't need a television.

BABCI: Lawrence Welk. Sometimes he plays Chopin.

CHOPIN: I'm right here. Am I dead?

MARYA: No. Chopin is not—we wait.

(BEEZO *enters.*)

BEEZO: What are you people waiting for?

CHOPIN: This woman waits for television, and this one needs—

BEEZO: Television. People need bread. People are hungry.

CHOPIN: I'm hungry for my music.

BEEZO: I'll join you.

MARYA: Get in line.

BEEZO: There should be no lines. People should have what they need. You don't see Beethoven on line.

CHOPIN: Mozart. There's another one who got away with murder. Tchaikovsky.

BEEZO: I could kill for a cup of coffee. (BEEZO *pulls out the hands of* CHOPIN. *One holds a cigar.*)

CHOPIN: Yes. Coffee. Have we met?

MARYA: And your piano. Don't forget.

BEEZO: Got a light?

(CHOPIN *lights her up.*)

BEEZO: There's a piano in Paris.

MARYA: She's breaking into line.

CHOPIN: Paris?

BEEZO: Yes. Paris. Where you belong. Painters like Delacroix. Writers like George Sand. Composers like Frederick Francois Chopin. There's action in Paris.

CHOPIN: I was on my way to Paris.

(STASH *enters.*)

STASH: There you are.

CHOPIN: Do I know you?

STASH: Stash. From the shipyard. In Gdansk.

CHOPIN: Stash?

STASH: We work together. The strike goes well. Solidarity.

CHOPIN: I'm a musician. You don't understand. I know nothing about—

STASH: I have pictures of the strike. And this is a picture. "The People Wait." Hold, please, for history. While I have my light. *(He shoots. He leaves.)*

BEEZO: We waste our time here.

CHOPIN: I was on my way to Paris. Excuse me. I have to go. We'll all meet here...again...tomorrow.

BEEZO: And, so! Welcome to Paris, my friend, City of Light. See the light?

CHOPIN: And heat. Feel the heat? *(Gunfire)*

BEEZO: And, so, now we find coffee at Cafe Voltaire, we find Delacroix, we have a big fight about whatever that foolish man is wrong about. But please be nice to him, Freddie. His pictures go badly, his commissions go poof.

CHOPIN: I am always nice to Delacroix. But if he talks politics...

BEEZO: Not without coffee, mon cheri. Ah, there is Delacroix.

*(DELACROIX enters.)*

BEEZO: Garçon! Coffee!

*(WAITER appears. Gunfire. The WAITER falls.)*

BEEZO: That is not our waiter.

CHOPIN: My good friend who uses bad color.

DELACROIX: My good friend with the broken fingers. *(They embrace.)*

BEEZO: Garçon! Coffee!

CHOPIN: Tell me: how go your paintings?

DELACROIX: There are things more important, mon ami. Today, I write in my journal: 28 July, 1830. A great day for Delacroix and France. I give up my summer light and meet with painters, poets, writers of the novel. The artists of Paris unite to stop the gunfire.

BEEZO: You waste your time with these people. You talk. On the streets of Paris people die. You help the royalists. Whose side are you on?

CHOPIN: I am glad you are kind to Delacroix.

BEEZO: I could kill for a cup of coffee. Garçon!

*(WAITER appears.)*

*(Gunfire. The WAITER falls.)*

BEEZO: This place is impossible. I get it myself. *(She exits.)*

CHOPIN: No, wait! You'll be killed!

DELACROIX: Impetuous woman.

CHOPIN: Who writes her books if something happens? And who makes your pictures.

DELACROIX: Sadly, no one makes my pictures. *(To a dying WAITER)* Don't worry, mon ami. We meet everyday to help you. *(Examining the man's blood)* I cannot use this color.

CHOPIN: Forgive me, mon ami. You waste your time with this.

*(BEEZO enters with a gun.)*

BEEZO: There is danger. There is no coffee. *(She exits.)*

CHOPIN: And her. "No one has coffee until everyone has coffee!" This concern with politics is all wrong, my friend. You sit in salons with idiots like yourself, and worse, that one, she picks up a gun.

DELACROIX: You are hard on us, my friend.

CHOPIN: I cherish your painting, not your politics. Make art. And that one, she'll get herself killed, mark my words. Or worse, she'll live to become the radical darling of Paris, a celebrity.

DELACROIX: We use our celebrity. We lend our names for the cause, we march on the Champs Elysees.

CHOPIN: No. Make your paintings. They have the magic your politics lack.

*(Gunfire. A WAITER enters. The WAITER is shot.)*

CHOPIN: What can I do but make music? Simple native tunes. We make beauty, you and I. They can't murder beauty.

DELACROIX: They do.

CHOPIN: They can't.

DELACROIX: They do.

CHOPIN: They can't.

DELACROIX: They do.

CHOPIN: They can't.

*(BEEZO enters barefoot, with gun.)*

CHOPIN: Come here and make love to me on this spot.

BEEZO: No. I win the coffee. Then we make love. (BEEZO *exits.*)

DELACROIX: Ah, that woman, she is like trying to paint the lightning.

CHOPIN: But paint her!

*(The wounded* WAITERS *are struggling toward the table.* MARYA *enters.)*

MARYA: Chopin, remember Poland!

CHOPIN: Where were we?

DELACROIX: You musicians speak the international language. Perfect for a time when there is fighting all over Europe.

MARYA: Chopin, Poland is lost! *(She exits.)*

CHOPIN: Did you say "all over Europe?"

DELACROIX: All over Europe.

CHOPIN: I dreamt I was in Poland. Russians attacked. Our soldiers danced the Polonaise on horseback. We were defeated. Women scattered flowers where brave men fell. Moscow is victorious. Moscow rules. Oh God, do you exist?

(BEEZO *unbloused, enters barefoot, but with coffee. She assumes a triumphant pose among the* WAITERS: *Liberty Guiding the People, 28 July, 1830 by Delacroix.)*

BEEZO: I found the coffee!

DELACROIX: Almost perfect. Almost perfect. Liberty, guiding the people! Today. 28 July, 1830! *(He replaces the coffee with a tricolor.)*

CHOPIN: And Poland, blessed Poland, lies dead at her feet. *(He swoons at her feet, in the picture.)*

FIRST WAITER: Liberté!

SECOND WAITER: Egalité!

THIRD WAITER: L'addition!

*(Blackout)*

CHOPIN: I long for Poland. Warszawa, the capital, is lovely this time of year. The sweetest smelling city in Europe. Broad streets, people drinking coffee along the Nowy Swiat. And trees, I don't know their names, but at this time in spring, in cloudless sunshine, with a gentle breeze from the west, our trees drop little white puffballs you can catch, kiss, and give to a lover. We call it spring snow, winter romance in the sunshine. *(Gentle "spring snow" falls.)* Like hope; so warm you want to remove your coat, your protection. Spring snow in Poland. *(The snow gets heavier.)* An illusion of winter, a beautiful dream.

*(The snow falls heavily. Blue lights.* CHOPIN *turns up his collar.* BEEZO *enters with travel literature, sees* CHOPIN *freezing in the snow.)*

BEEZO: What are you waiting for?

CHOPIN: Polish spring.

BEEZO: This is no place for you. You're freezing. We get some vacation.

CHOPIN: No, I am needed.

BEEZO: Come, Freddie, we leave all this behind. We go to Majorca.

CHOPIN: I'm going to die of consumption. *(Cough)*

BEEZO: Don't be ridiculous. We don't have to stay here.

CHOPIN: I dreamt I was in Poland. *(Cough)*

BEEZO: We go to Majorca. We make a big holiday. Artists need vacation, too. There is water like emerald, sky like turquoise. And cactus, this is how dry it is, good for your cold.

CHOPIN: Consumption. I am consumed.

BEEZO: So, I feed, you consume.

CHOPIN: I am consumed by Poland.

BEEZO: When we get your piano, you will forget everything else and make your music.

CHOPIN: My music.

BEEZO: It's all been arranged. Look how lovely. Sunshine? Sea?

CHOPIN:I want to take the simple country tunes of my native.... *(Coughs)*

BEEZO: See? This weather helps you. You cough better. I go into town, I find your piano. Enjoy the sun, mon amour, and dream of my return.

*(*BEEZO *exits.* CHOPIN *coughs.* CHOPIN *paces.* CHOPIN's *funeral dirge.* CHOPIN *paces and coughs. He sees visions of Poland.* BEEZO *returns.)*

CHOPIN: Where is my piano?

BEEZO: The letter says it's being put on a cargo vessel in Marseilles.

CHOPIN: Great. It's going to sit in the harbor all winter and I won't get anything done. This place is a disaster. Where's the sun? *(He coughs.)* Poland is lost.

BEEZO: The weather will change.

CHOPIN: All I hear is raindrops and death marches. I'm hungry for my music.

BEEZO: Oh, and it's my fault.

CHOPIN: I'm not blaming you.

BEEZO: Of course you do. It's my fault the weather's bad. It's my fault they don't deliver your piano.

(CHOPIN *coughs*.)

CHOPIN: I'm losing my life here.

BEEZO: Don't be dramatic.

CHOPIN: I'm Christ on a cross here. My hands are bound.

(*A* TANK *rumbles across*.)

CHOPIN: How do we stop that?

BEEZO: Stop what?

CHOPIN: Why am I cursed with this? He'll kill you. He'll kill us both.

BEEZO: Chopin, you're dreaming.

CHOPIN: We stand or fall by the music. (*He coughs*.) You promised me a piano. You promised me some peace and serenity.

(TANK *re-rumbles. This time,* BEEZO *notices*.)

BEEZO: So, the honeymoon is over.

(*She exits. The* TANK *follows*.)

CHOPIN: Father, if this be your will...(*He has a coughing fit*.) How can this be your will?

(*Blackout*)

(MARYA *enters, chased by what she thinks is the* BEAR. *She turns to see it's only the* POPE.)

MARYA: Oh, Holy Father! I thought you were someone else. Chopin, I was wondering. Could you meet with Holy Father and tell him our troubles, you know, how the bear comes, I must smack in the nose and we make music when all is nice? Chopin, you don't look so good.

CHOPIN: It's nothing. Holy Father, we need help.

POPE: You catch me at a bad time. Poland, too. The only free Poland is in that bit of dirt Marya gave you.

CHOPIN: I never got it.

(MARYA *smiles sheepishly and hands him some soil*.)

MARYA: So sorry. We're running out of Poland. We must save.

(CHOPIN *holds soil to his ear and listens*.)

CHOPIN: It's very quiet.

*(The* POPE *grabs the soil, blesses it, and eats it.)*

POPE: I'll take that. Listen, Lech.

CHOPIN: Frederick.

POPE: Did I see you in church this week?

CHOPIN: I was in Majorca. I'll come next week.

POPE: Good. Now, I can't come out and say "do this" or "do that" because my kingdom is not of this world, understand? The bear—

MARYA: Deserves a smack in the nose.

POPE: The bear's not the problem.

CHOPIN: I dream differently. *(Coughs)*

POPE: Let us pray. He won't interrupt prayer. I have his word.

*(*BABCI *enters.)*

BABCI: Excuse, please. Is this the end of the line?

CHOPIN: I hope not.

BABCI: Excuse, please. Where is?

*(*CHOPIN *coughs a lot.)*

BABCI: It's okay.

POPE: I can't stay. You understand. *(He exits.)*

BABCI: Was that the pope?

CHOPIN: Yes.

BABCI: He was here?

MARYA: Yes, he was here.

BABCI: I don't feel any different.

*(*STASH *enters.)*

STASH: Boy, I want a picture of this.

BABCI: Don't mind me.

CHOPIN: What are you doing?

STASH: *(Shooting pictures)* No, we want everybody in the pictures. When the people see this... look over here! Wait till they see this.

CHOPIN: I'll wait here until I get my piano. And these brave people are brave enough to wait with me.

STASH: One more. You all look at your leader. Who's the leader?

CHOPIN: We are a people together, we act as one. We have no leader. Just people together, citizens of Poland. Brave people.

*(Beeping starts. The* BEAR *enters and stands between* MARYA *and* CHOPIN, *just trying to get in the picture.* MARYA *doesn't notice who it is.)*

MARYA: Hey, he's breaking into the —uh–oh...get out of the way.

*(The* BEAR *squeezes* CHOPIN *and* MARYA.*)*

MARYA: I said get away!

*(She smacks the* BEAR *on the nose. The* BEAR *chases her out.)*

STASH: Got it. Good.

CHOPIN: Just a minute. What are these pictures, and what are you going to do with them? What are these pictures for? May I have that camera?

*(*BEEZO *enters and sizes up the situation.)*

BEEZO: What are you waiting for? *(She smashes the camera.)*

STASH: Hey, what are you doing?

BEEZO: He's working for the government.

STASH: You're out of your mind. *(His camera ruined, he pulls out a mini camera and continues snapping.)*

CHOPIN: You're back.

*(*BEEZO *gives him a peck on the cheek.)*

BABCI: Don't mind me.

*(*CHOPIN, *embarrassed, indicates they should be respectful of* BABCI. BEEZO *and* CHOPIN *whisper in each other's ears.* STASH *films this. The beeps continue.* STASH *busts* BEEZO.*)*

STASH: Perfect. Let's go. Okay, that's enough. I said, that's enough. You have exactly ten seconds to disperse.

CHOPIN: No. We stand together, citizens of Poland. We affirm our right to assemble freely, to articulate our grievances. Did I say that?

STASH: What's the nature of your grievance?

CHOPIN: My piano. I mean to play for Poland. It's missing.

STASH: And you blame the state?

CHOPIN: I blame the persons responsible.

STASH: Your ten seconds are up. Over here.

CHOPIN: I'm not leaving.

STASH: Please. Be reasonable. For your own good.

CHOPIN: No.

(STASH *shoves* CHOPIN *over to where* BEEZO'S *been placed.* STASH *exits.*)

BEEZO: What are you here for?

CHOPIN: I beg your pardon?

BEEZO: Why did they arrest you?

CHOPIN: I haven't been arrested.

BEEZO: Hah. Being held without charge.

CHOPIN: Don't worry. This is just a misunderstanding. I'm a famous composer.

BEEZO: Not here. Here, they treat you like dirt. I don't trust that man.

CHOPIN: Don't worry. He's a Pole. A countryman. This is just a misunderstanding. He knows what side he's on.

(STASH *enters.*)

STASH: You're Lech?

CHOPIN: Frederick. There's a misunderstanding.

STASH: It's me. Stash. Would you excuse us for a moment?

BEEZO: No.

CHOPIN: Let her stay.

STASH: No problem. I just thought she might want some coffee. There's coffee in the other room.

BEEZO: Coffee? There's coffee?

(*She exits.* STASH *pours drinks for himself and* CHOPIN. *They drink once. Twice.* STASH *pours himself and* CHOPIN *a drink. They drink. He pours another round. They drink again.*)

STASH: Sto lat.

CHOPIN: There isn't any coffee.

STASH: Don't worry about it.

CHOPIN: Where did you send her?

STASH: It's not your problem. You were looking for a piano.

CHOPIN: Yes. I know I can help Poland.

(STASH *pours. They drink.*)

STASH: Sto lat. No one gets a piano until everyone gets a piano. I make a joke. It would be a very difficult move to the front of the line if these pictures were to be made public. How I love that summer light.

CHOPIN: Let me see those. *(He takes the pictures.)* I did nothing wrong.

STASH: Of course not. Artistic license. Laws don't apply to you. Just ordinary people. I didn't touch her. Show me where I touched her.

CHOPIN: I would like assurance that nothing happens to that woman.

STASH: In the old days, she wouldn't be sent off for coffee. She'd be sent off to be de-loused. Those were the days. When Poles can't solve their problems, we get help from our neighbors.

CHOPIN: Whose side are you on?

STASH: Whose side are you on, Lech?

*(He pours. They drink.)*

STASH: Sto lat.

CHOPIN: Do you have my piano?

STASH: Of course.

*(He pours. CHOPIN doesn't drink.)*

STASH: You're not drinking.

CHOPIN: What's in this?

STASH: Good Polish Vodka.

CHOPIN: My music.

STASH: Friend, you've already made your music.

CHOPIN: The strike. It goes well? The shipyard? Gdansk?

STASH: I tell you, those troublemakers have been liberated. Drink up.

*(CHOPIN throws drink down.)*

CHOPIN: I don't trust you.

STASH: Your own countryman? You see me in church. You don't see her in church.

CHOPIN: I want...assurance....

*(He gets up. He tries to walk. He falls. STASH takes his picture.)*

STASH: One hell of a leader.

*(Blackout)*

*(CHOPIN sleeps. The BEAR and the TANK appear. HITLER gets out of the TANK.)*

*(HITLER and the BEAR each have a hand of CHOPIN: They shake. The BEAR grabs HITLER's hand and claps the two together clumsily but vigorously. HITLER sets up his easel and begins drawing these:)*

*(He hangs them on a clothesline, advancing them across the stage as they are finished. CHOPIN awakes and indignantly takes the hands from the BEAR, who exits sorrowfully.)*

CHOPIN: This isn't happening. I'm dreaming.

*(BEEZO and MARYA enter from opposite places.)*

MARYA & BEEZO: The hands of Chopin!

*(They make a dash for the hands and pull CHOPIN in opposite directions. The POPE enters.)*

POPE: Now, let's get our theology straight. There's God, and there's man.

CHOPIN: And I'm in the middle.

POPE: Render unto Caesar? Thou shalt have no graven images?

*(POPE gives hands to BEEZO.)*

BEEZO: They're practically ruined! *(She exits.)*

POPE: We have Our Lord and His Holy Mother.

MARYA: Catch the Jew! *(She notices the TANKS.)* Holy Father, we need Chopin to stop the tanks.

CHOPIN: No, I'm not here.

POPE: We don't need hands.

MARYA: Maybe the heart of Chopin?

POPE: No, not that.

MARYA: Nostradamus?

POPE: He was a heretic.

MARYA: How about the Black Madonna, Queen of Poland, who saved us from the Swedes?

POPE: I'm sorry; we can't use the Black Madonna.

CHOPIN: Why not?

MARYA: You remember? She save us in 1282, when all is lost. Soldiers hold up picture, lots of smoke, big mess, Swedes run away?

POPE: But the Black Madonna is not available for this miracle.

CHOPIN: This isn't my dream. This isn't happening.

MARYA: We are Chosen People, no, Holy Father?

POPE: Sorry. Not this time.

CHOPIN: Stash has my piano. I'm waiting for Stash. That's it. *(He goes back to sleep.)*

MARYA: Holy Father, I'm no good with needle and thread. Maybe I be Holy Mother, like on Christmas. I stop tanks. You help.

POPE: How can I help? *(He blesses her.)* Good luck. *(He exits.)*

CHOPIN: My dream is music and beauty. This couldn't be my dream.

*(The TANKS come closer. MARYA puts on a Black Madonna costume. Crown, halo, child. She blackens her face.)*

MARYA: I stand like this, right, Holy Father? I save Poland.

*(BABCI throws flowers where tanks have passed. MARYA hums a hymn. She hums Chopin. She hums patriotic songs.)*

MARYA: Stop. Stop.

*(MARYA can't stop the TANKS. BEEZO enters with the hands and a yellow Star of David as these emerge from HITLER's easel:)*

BEEZO: They said pack quickly. They didn't say how long.

*(They converge on BEEZO, BABCI, and MARYA.)*

MARYA: Holy Father! *(She runs off, into the arms of the BEAR.)*

CHOPIN: Poles die. And I am helpless. Warszawa is silent. And I am helpless. The Old Town is destroyed. And I am helpless. The Jews trapped in the ghetto. And I am helpless. The church where my heart is placed in an urn—

*(Blackout)*

*(CHOPIN alone on stage.)*

CHOPIN: Was I acquainting you with the circumstances of my death? Place Vendome? Paris? Two A M? The 17th of October?

*(Blackout)*

*(BEEZO is locked in a cage. HITLER stands at his easel as if at a lectern. He writes the word)*

# SOLUTIONS

*(on the sketch pad.)*

HITLER: Our lesson for today begins with a riddle. Question: why did the chicken cross the road? Answer: to get to the other side. However: to get to the other side, he had to get through...

*(HITLER tears a page off the sketch pad to reveal:)*

HITLER: Poland! Ha-ha-ha-ha! Riddle. Punchline. Solution. *(He throws "Poland" on the floor.)* And how do we get through this Poland?

*(He draws yet another tank. CHOPIN approaches HITLER.)*

CHOPIN: What are these things?

HITLER: Tanks.

CHOPIN: I had a dream about these tanks. They came to Poland. I played the Polonaise. They destroyed my country.

HITLER: Shut up and feed the Jew.

CHOPIN: I beg your pardon?

HITLER: The one who took your piano. She sleeps with the bear.

BEEZO: That's not true!

(CHOPIN *approaches* BEEZO. *He kisses her hand.*)

CHOPIN: Mademoiselle...

BEEZO: Oh, no, Chopin. It is your hands that must be adored. Remember these? (*She shows him the hands.*)

CHOPIN: Wait a minute. Have we met?

BEEZO: Paris. We sat for our friend, Eugene Delacroix. I was Liberty, Guiding the People.

CHOPIN: July 28, 1830! We were in Paris together. We were safe.

BEEZO: At Rue de Grenelle. We ate at Café Voltaire. We are no longer safe.

CHOPIN: What are you doing here?

BEEZO: This madman will kill me.

CHOPIN: Why?

BEEZO: Because I am a Jew.

CHOPIN: That's ridiculous.

HITLER: Don't listen to her. Jew, Gypsy, it makes no difference.

CHOPIN: I'd like assurance that nothing happens to this woman. She's beauty, liberty; she's fire, patriotism.

(HITLER *knocks* CHOPIN *to the ground.*)

HITLER: Don't push me, Polish boy.

(CHOPIN *takes a picture of a tank and tears it up. He takes the "Poland" map and* HITLER's *pencil, drawing furiously on the map.*)

HITLER: May I draw?!

(MARYA *enters.*)

MARYA: Chopin, that woman is trouble! Don't bother with her. (*She exits.*)

HITLER: Whose side are you on? We artists have to stick together, no? What are you unless you make music? What am I unless I draw a tank? Cage a Jew? Nicht wahr?

CHOPIN: You murder beauty. This woman is a piece of art. *(He holds up the piece of paper, which he has made into:)*

CHOPIN: This! This is what I need. This is how I stop you.

*(MARYA enters.)*

MARYA: Play, Chopin! Play for Poland! *(She exits.)*

HITLER: Useless Pole! This is bad art. I ask for Wagner, they send me Chopin!

*(HITLER grabs the plaster hands from BEEZO.)*

HITLER: Is this your solution? Huh? *(He plays the hands on the piano. Crude, atonal music. The hands begin bleeding. They bleed all over the drawing.)*

CHOPIN: Dear holy country, how he mocks you. In my dream Poland lives, Poland sings. My piano sings for Poland! *(He returns to BEEZO.)* We sailed to Majorca.

BEEZO: Yes.

CHOPIN: We'll go back.

BEEZO: We can't.

CHOPIN: It's only a bad dream. We'll wake up in Majorca.

*(He removes her from the cage. They flee. MARYA enters.)*

MARYA: Where is my Cho—Dear Savior. What happened?

HITLER: He took my Jew to Majorca. Look at this mess.

MARYA: Herr Hitler, forgive us. *(She exits and returns with a pail and a scrub brush. She scrubs the drawing.)* This must never be. What are people going to say when they see such a mess? We're not like the others. *(She spits toward the cage.)* We're clean and honest people. How could such a thing happen? Forgive us, forgive my Chopin. Did he steal your Jew? Don't worry, I know where there's more. You see what happens? This was a nice, clean Poland. I shouldn't let this kind of thing happen. What else? *(She has inadvertently shredded the drawing. Poland in shreds.)*

HITLER: Stupid woman! Look what you've done.

MARYA: What have I done?

HITLER: All because of a Jew. You couldn't leave well enough alone. He's left you for that Jude. You want to go in there, huh?

*(MARYA tries to gather up the shredded drawing.)*

HITLER: See whose hands are covered with blood? Not mine. *(He holds up the hands.)*

MARYA: I would cross Europe on my knees to kiss those hands.

*(HITLER throws MARYA into the cage and exits in pursuit of BEEZO. The POPE enters.)*

POPE: Just a minute. What did I tell you about this?

MARYA: They're not Hitler's hands. They're the hands of Chopin.

*(The POPE releases her from the cage.)*

POPE: Come on. This is no place for you. Now: render unto Caesar? My kingdom is not of this world? Thou shalt have no graven images unto Me?

MARYA: Chopin will help us.

POPE: The Lord has a plan.

MARYA: No! Nostradamus has a plan. He says the next time, everyone will perish and the Poles will triumph!

*(BEEZO enters, prisoner of HITLER. She is caged. The POPE offers her the hands.)*

POPE: These are yours?

BEEZO: No.

*(The POPE shrugs. BABCI scatters flowers. CHOPIN approaches BABCI.)*

CHOPIN: I have this bad dream, see. I want to tell you about it.

*(HITLER invites MARYA to dance. The BEAR springs BEEZO free and invites her to dance.)*

CHOPIN: I don't know quite how to tell you, since it's about people very close to me.

*(The couples dance.)*

CHOPIN: They do terrible things to my music. They ask me to play simple native tunes of my homeland. I sit. I play. They dance. And I am helpless. I can't believe they dance together. I try to stop. My fingers won't stop. I can't stop my hands. They make me play on. They're not my hands. *(He grabs the bloody hands, now abandoned.)* I hope you forgive me if I don't tell you these dreams, for I fear they'll come true. These terrible dreams that I have about my loved ones. *(He breaks the hands.)* Forgive me.

*(STASH is now on stage. The dancers have vanished.)*

STASH: For what?

CHOPIN: Thinking the worst.

STASH: Thinking's no crime.

CHOPIN: Just a figure of speech.

STASH: Thinking the worst is a crime, though. Your aspirations are the aspirations of the people. When you think the worst you create negativity in the state. That's a crime. I'm just telling you this for your own good.

CHOPIN: This is just a bad dream.

STASH: Then wake up.

*(The dream ends. Blackout)*

*(CHOPIN and MARYA, idly.)*

MARYA: Chopin, I was—

CHOPIN: Wondering?

MARYA: What?

CHOPIN: Yes. What. To do. Who our friends are?

*(BEEZO enters on a bicycle.)*

BEEZO: Telegram for Mr Chopin. Frederick Chopin.

CHOPIN: What is it?

BEEZO: Telegram.

*(MARYA and BEEZO eye each other hard.)*

CHOPIN: *(Reading)* "Congratulations on assuming control of Poland's destiny. Stop. You have my one hundred per cent support. Stop. Your enemies are my enemies. Stop. Let's talk. Signed, The President of the United States."

MARYA: Oh my Chopin. We go to Washington!

BEEZO: You going like that?

*(MARYA does a small curtsey.)*

MARYA: Excuse, please, my Chopin.

*(She exits.* CHOPIN *makes to follow.)*

BEEZO: Wait a minute. There's more.

CHOPIN: "P S: We can make some beautiful music." They must have my piano. Of course. We'll sing for Poland in America. If a man needs music, he finds it in America. Who's president now?

BEEZO: Doesn't matter. Their policy is bipartisan.

CHOPIN: This is a good dream. America!

BEEZO: It's a wonderful dream. You'll play in the White House, there'll be a dinner in your honor. A press conference in the Rose Garden. Then a tour: recitals in New York, Chicago, Los Angeles.

CHOPIN: This is very nice, but this is a visit. I don't go to stay.

BEEZO: Mr Chopin, you want Liberace to do your music? You're immortal. When Americans go to the movies, they'll see you on the newsreel.

CHOPIN: You don't understand. I seek help for my country. When Americans had their revolution, we helped. Now, they have a chance to help us.

*(The* BEAR, *eavesdropping, has been getting closer.)*

CHOPIN: Freedom loving Americans and freedom loving Poles. This is the greatest dream of all. There's a bear behind you.

BEEZO: Oh. It's all right. Don't worry. He's my friend.

CHOPIN: I don't trust him.

BEEZO: He's just a bear. Say hello to the famous composer.

*(The* BEAR *offers a paw.)*

BEEZO: See? He likes you. There's nothing to be afraid of.

CHOPIN: He likes you.

BEEZO: Of course he does. He likes you. No paws. No paws. What have you got for Mommie?

CHOPIN: I still don't trust him.

BEEZO: He's got a telegram. For someone named Lech.

CHOPIN: I'd better take that. *(He reads.)* "Don't go to Washington unless accompanied by the bearer of this message. Let him do all the talking. He knows what's best for you." This is highly unlikely. Who wrote this message?

BEEZO: It's not signed.

CHOPIN: Who's this from?

*(The* BEAR *shrugs.)*

CHOPIN: Are you the one who's been chasing Marya around?

*(The* BEAR *shakes his head "no.")*

CHOPIN: Are you sure?

*(The* BEAR *nods his head "yes.")*

CHOPIN: Are you stupid? Do you know what I'm saying? I don't trust him.

*(The* BEAR *shrugs.)*

BEEZO: He's just a bear.

CHOPIN: No. If he comes to America we're lost. I must make a case for my country.

BEEZO: For everyone. A case for all of Europe. We'll all go together.

CHOPIN: No, I'll go alone.

BEEZO: You're making a big mistake. Come on, baby.

CHOPIN: No. You're making the mistake. Don't trust the bear!

*(*BEEZO *and the* BEAR *exit.* MARYA *enters with a new hat, eggs, a sword and the record.)*

MARYA: Is so busy, shopping for the trip.

*(A scream offstage)*

MARYA: What was that?

*(The* BEAR *bicycles by.)*

CHOPIN: I'll go to America. Goodbye!

MARYA: Talk to Mr Roosevelt. He save us from the you-know-who. And...

*(Blackout)*

MARYA: I'll come with you. I'll bring eggs.

CHOPIN: You weren't invited.

MARYA: That's okay. I bring my own food. Take this sword.
Tell Mr Roosevelt you'll help him fight your common enemies.

CHOPIN: My music will stop the tanks, Mr Roosevelt.

*(Music is heard.* HARRY TRUMAN *enters playing "Hail to the Chief" in a jaunty Chico Marx impersonation.)*

CHOPIN: That's not my music. Excuse me...

HARRY: Uh-uh. You can't come in here.

CHOPIN: Mr Roosevelt?

HARRY: Mr Truman. Mr Roosevelt's watching *Duck Soup*.

CHOPIN: We're from Poland.

HARRY: I'm from Missouri. You can't come in unless you know the password.

CHOPIN: Password? We know nothing about a password.

HARRY: I give you a hint. It's the name of a fish. Haddock.

CHOPIN: Haddock?

HARRY: Atsa funny. I got a haddock, too. Hahaha.

MARYA: I'm sorry. Our English is not so good.

CHOPIN: Now can I see the president?

HARRY: He's watching a movie.

CHOPIN: What's a movie?

HARRY: It's a *Duck Soup*.

MARYA: Could I see a movie?

(HARRY *lets* MARYA *in, who races off.*)

HARRY: You wait here.

CHOPIN: Did I hear a piano before? Is it mine?

HARRY: You have to talk to the president. He's a with the Allies. Everybody's watching the Marx Brothers.

(ELEANOR *enters, in the manner of Margaret Dumont.*)

ELEANOR: Ah, sir, welcome to America, land of the free!

HARRY: And home of the Boston Braves. She's the wife of the head cheese.

(CHOPIN *kisses her hand.*)

CHOPIN: Gracious lady, we seek your assistance.

ELEANOR: How lovely. You'll have to bring it up with Franklin. Franklin! Franklin!

(MARYA *enters, distressed, pursued by the* BEAR, *who is dressed like Harpo Marx. He honks a horn. They exit.* HARRY *plays Captain Spaulding music for F D R, who enters smoking a cigar.*)

F D R: Take a letter.

HARRY: To who?

F D R: The Polish government. Dear Polish Government: Enclosed please find a check for five million dollars. Send that off immediately.

CHOPIN: Thank you!

HARRY: I'll have to enclose the check first.

F D R: You do and I'll fire you. Go to Congress. Ride like fury. If you run out of gas, get ethyl. If ethyl runs out, get Mabel. Now, step on it.

(HARRY *exits.*)

F D R: We never travel together. Security.

ELEANOR: Franklin, Franklin. I want to present to you the Ambassador from Poland. Having you stay with us is a great pleasure.

CHOPIN: But I can't stay.

F D R: That's even a greater pleasure.

CHOPIN: I came for my piano. Is that it?

F D R: Like this cigar? It's a good quarter cigar. I smoked the other three quarters an hour ago.

CHOPIN: Sir, you try my patience.

F D R: Don't mind if I do. You must come over and try mine some time.

CHOPIN: Mr President, please. This telegram came for me. It said you would help us. I must play my music. Your enemies are my enemies.

(F D R *takes the telegram.*)

F D R: Huh. Why, a four-year-old child could understand this. Run out and get me a four-year-old child. On the other hand, I have five fingers. Now, let's see what I have in my cabinet besides mice.

(F D R *exits.*)

ELEANOR: How he loves the Marx Brothers!

(MARYA *enters.*)

CHOPIN: Marya!

MARYA: No problem. Where was I? Excuse me, please, Mrs Roosevelt, this is...this man, he symbolizes Poland, and...I bring eggs. We paint design and pictures. For you.

ELEANOR: And what are the eggs a symbol of?

MARYA: Our Saviour. He's like Poland. He dies. Gets up. Saves everybody.

ELEANOR: So, your saviour is inside the egg?

MARYA: No, he's outside. This man...I'm sorry, my English is not so good. We make a hole on top and a hole on a bottom and blow him out. It makes me so lightheaded! Then we paint the outside and we sing hymns. Mostly, we don't know the words so we just hum.

ELEANOR: And the swordsman?

CHOPIN: Marya.

MARYA: No, please, my Chopin. He makes music and he saves our country. When the tanks come, Radio Poland plays the Polonaise every hour so the world knows Poland is not yet dead. There is very beautiful. Is everywhere: Chopin in Warszawa, Chopin in Paris, Chopin in space, drifting out, so far. I am sorry I am not Copernicus. I don't know where my Chopin goes sometimes.

CHOPIN: The music stops the tanks, yes.

MARYA: We show. Please, give now the record.

CHOPIN: Yes.

(*He searches for the record in his pockets.* MARYA *pulls the record from his chest.*)

MARYA: Dear Chopin, is by your heart.

(CHOPIN *makes circling motions with his sword as* MARYA *hums a tune and spins the record with her finger beneath the point of the sword.*)

MARYA: I'm so sorry; we are a poor country.

ELEANOR: I'm sure Franklin would like you to perform.

CHOPIN: On my piano!

ELEANOR: I'm afraid we don't have your piano. My husband used to take me on moonlight cruises and serenade me with this. (*She offers* CHOPIN *a ukelele.*)

CHOPIN: No, I need a piano.

(F D R *enters.*)

ELEANOR: Look what they brought us, dear. A recording.

(*The* BEAR, *still Harpo, enters.*)

F D R: A three record set.

(*The* BEAR *honks and growls.* F D R *gives him a record.*)

F D R: A two record set.

(*The* BEAR *honks.* F D R *gives him a record.*)

F D R: It's no good anyway. It's got a hole in it.

(*The* BEAR *honks and growls.* F D R *give him the last record.*)

F D R: Have I sung "Hello, I must be going?"

CHOPIN: What have you done?

F D R: What are you going to do? He's a bear.

(*The* BEAR *exits, happy.*)

F D R: You can't hate an ally who loves the Marx Brothers. (*He is himself again.*) Now, what's this about a little music?

CHOPIN: You've taken my music and given it away.

F D R: This is America. There's plenty of music. Dear, do you have my ukelele?

ELEANOR: Here it is.

F D R: Eleanor plays the slide trombone. And if this dear lady...

MARYA: Mostly hum.

F D R: Yes. Something like *I'm Always Chasing Rainbows.* Remember that one?

ELEANOR: Such fun.

(*They play.* MARYA *hums along.*)

CHOPIN: I don't need accompaniment. And it's not *I'm Always Chasing Rainbows.* It's my Impromptu #4 in C Sharp Minor, Opus 66, which I composed nearly one hundred and fifty years ago. Now, through the miracle of the recording industry, it's gone. You gave it away. You gave it all away.

MARYA: Please, I apologize for my Chopin.

CHOPIN: No.

MARYA: Yes. He makes music of our homeland, but it isn't so good in big group. He must play by himself.

F D R: Well. Sorry to hear. I guess you don't need us. God Bless!

(F D R *and* ELEANOR *exit.*)

MARYA: My Chopin, I must apologize. I make a big mess.

CHOPIN: No. No. You were fine. We shouldn't have trusted them. We shouldn't trust any of them.

(*Blackout*)

(CHOPIN *alone. He lies on no one's lap.*)

CHOPIN: Marya, I was wondering. Chopin, I was wondering. What? Do you think? I mean, you know, do you think, our native country homeland? Do you think a year in jail, you know, simple country songs of our native homeland, will drive this stupid idea out of your head? Do you think you'll stop having dreams about calling our movement, you know,

Solidarity, and shipworkers, you know, actors and farmers into something the world will love? Dignity for our people and a piano, to let Poland sing for Poland? Do you think your heart can sing for Poland, your breast beat for Poland, a small packet of earth carried with you mean that Poland is with you, even if, you know, you don't know how to make your music?

*(Blackout)*

*(*CHOPIN *asleep.* BABCI *enters with flowers. Tatty flowers.* CHOPIN *awakes with a start.)*

BABCI: Forgive me. The street in our village is named in your honor.
*(She gives him the flowers.)*

CHOPIN: Thank you. They're lovely.

BABCI: No. It's all we have. We plant crops, but there are no tractors. So we harvest flowers. Bugs come from the east, we look to the west for bug killer. Nothing.

CHOPIN: They're very lovely. If I had my piano, I would put them in music.

BABCI: Water's good. Not tap water.

CHOPIN: May I give you something for them?

*(He puts the flowers down and searches his pocket. A young woman in black enters with flowers, weeping. She places her flowers on the other flowers, sobs, and exits. A gentleman enters with a flower in his lapel and places it with the others. He shows* CHOPIN *the inside of his lapel and exits. The* POPE *enters. He kisses the ground.* MARYA *enters, sees the* POPE, *and lays flowers at his feet. She stands behind* BABCI, *making a line.* STASH *enters in uniform, ceremoniously carrying an official wreath. He sets it on a tripod where the other flowers lie. The* POPE *exits. The* BEAR *enters.)*

STASH: Of course you have a permit.

CHOPIN: For what?

STASH: This is government property. You'll have to move.

CHOPIN: Why?

STASH: Please, Lech, you understand. This isn't my decision. You'll all have to move.

CHOPIN: But the Pope...

STASH: Yes. The Pope. Lech, I feel terrible about it, really. But we're concerned about your safety. Safety requires that citizens stay away from open trenches.

CHOPIN: But there aren't any open trenches.

STASH: They're being installed this evening. Soldiers will be posted to prevent vandalism.

*(The* BEAR *exits.)*

STASH: After construction is finished, you can meet again. You have my word.

CHOPIN: When will that be?

*(*STASH *shrugs. The* POPE *enters.* STASH *gives him a plane.)*

STASH: Holy Father, before you return to Rome, give me your blessing.

*(The* POPE *blesses* STASH *and exits with the plane. A gunshot is heard. The* BEAR *enters with smoking gun and exits through the flowers.)*

STASH: If you would be so good as to come with me.

CHOPIN: Where are you taking me?

STASH: Please. For your own safety. Orders require.

CHOPIN: We have a right to be here!

*(*STASH *busts* CHOPIN.*)*

CHOPIN: All right! The party's over. Get a move on. Break it up.

*(*STASH *and others exit.* BEEZO *enters.)*

BEEZO: What are you waiting for?

CHOPIN: I can't do this myself.

BEEZO: Go to America. Meet the president.

CHOPIN: Oh, no. I've tried that once.

BEEZO: America is where dreams come true.

CHOPIN: Bad dreams, too.

BEEZO: Times change. Presidents change. You were right about the bear. We're on your side now. What's good for Poland is good for the world. Just tell the president your dream. He believes in dreams.

CHOPIN: I wish I could believe you.

BEEZO: America is the world capital of dreams, and this president is from the capital of America. The entertainment capital.

CHOPIN: The last one was a very bad dream.

BEEZO: Bad movie. You found yourself in a bad movie, and that happens from time to time. But you're going to be in a good movie, one with a happy ending. You're very popular in America. Want to see?

*(*CHOPIN DOUBLE *enters with record.)*

CHOPIN DOUBLE: Hi there! My name is Frederick Chopin. The music you hear in the background. Sound familiar? Perhaps you recognize it as that great popular hit, *Could It Be Magic*, by Barry Manilow. But not many of you may realize that *Could It Be Magic*, by Barry Manilow, is actually the melody from my Prelude #20 in C Minor, Opus 28, a piece of music I composed nearly one hundred and fifty years ago. Now, through the miracle of the recording industry, this great tune and more are yours, available in this great album.

BEEZO: Thank you.

(CHOPIN DOUBLE *exits.*)

BEEZO: See? Wait here. *(She exits.)*

CHOPIN: Just a moment. What can I do but present our case? What can I ask but that people are just? What can I lose but my life?

(REAGAN *enters.*)

REAGAN: Draw!

CHOPIN: What?

REAGAN: Hah. It's not real. Just giving you the finger.

(CHOPIN *gives the Solidarity sign.*)

REAGAN: Put that away. I've got something better. It's a story about a man and his music. You're going to get your piano. And get the girl. She's around here somewhere.

(BEEZO *enters as Nancy Reagan.*)

REAGAN: That's my girl. Hi, Mommie.

CHOPIN: Have we met?

BEEZO: I've heard your music, so I feel that we have.

REAGAN: Heck, that's why we think you should be in the business.

CHOPIN: What business?

BEEZO: Show business.

REAGAN: Why, in just two movies during the last war, and I served with a lot of good fellas from every country—do you know Kirk Douglas? I think he's a Polish fella. I served with him over at Warner Brothers. And I got the girl.

CHOPIN: Liberace?

REAGAN: What's that?

BEEZO: We're going to help you out.

REAGAN: You want to get the girl?

CHOPIN: I want to sit down with our leaders and plan a just society, free of outside interference.

REAGAN: If you do good, you'll get the girl. Now, the only thing is a screen test.

CHOPIN: A screen test?

REAGAN: You just stand up there and act natural. Just play out a little something from your experience that the world will love. You can make it up. Heck, I'm making this up.

(MARYA *enters*.)

REAGAN: Here's the girl, and you can win her over if you're right for the part. Just show us a little scene. Lights!

(*Blackout*)

REAGAN: Lights! (*Lights come up again.*) Camera! Rolling!

CHOPIN: This is a farewell scene, one between a heroic laborer who seeks a better life for his fellow Pole—

REAGAN: And his girl?

CHOPIN: I'll play the hero. His name is Lech. I've been arrested because I'm a troublemaker. Marya will play his wife, Danuta. In this scene, Lech is going to prison. I'm packing for the trip, I don't know how long I'll be away. Did I say they have six children, another on the way? We do. And the country's in a terrible way, because instead of manufacturing designer jeans for export like the Hungarians do, our leaders have decided that what the world needs is golf carts. So they turn three tractor plants over to the manufacture of golf carts. Golf carts. We can't plant crops because we have no tractors. But we have golf carts.

MARYA: Could we get on with the scene, please?

CHOPIN: How many of you play golf? How many of you own a golf cart? How many of you own a pair of designer jeans? Do you know how much it costs to ship a golf cart across the ocean?

MARYA: Chopin!

CHOPIN: Just a minute.

MARYA: The Americans don't want to hear about our problems. Let's just do the scene.

CHOPIN: The scene is about our problems. I'm giving them background.

MARYA: I must apologize for Mr Chopin.

CHOPIN: You can put—

MARYA: Frederick!

CHOPIN: —four people in one golf cart, and every one of them could be wearing a pair of designer jeans made in Hungary. Even if just two of them—

MARYA: They don't want to hear about it.

CHOPIN: Okay. We'll do the scene. Here I am in my fourteenth floor apartment in Gdansk, a bunch of newsmen outside, in a last few moments with my wife.

MARYA: And you don't know when you're going to see her again.

CHOPIN: That's right. So, here we are....

MARYA: Did you pack your socks?

CHOPIN: Yes.

MARYA: Don't pack the yellow socks. When they go through your drawers at night they'll see the holes in your socks and wonder what kind of wife you have.

CHOPIN: No. They'll wonder what kind of revolution they have, where the leader has holes in his socks.

MARYA: It's a reflection on me.

CHOPIN: No it isn't.

MARYA: It is, too.

CHOPIN: It's a reflection on a system that doesn't allow a man to throw out his socks when they get holes.

MARYA: I know you're going to make a big thing out of it and show those socks to the western newsmen. Don't embarrass me that way.

CHOPIN: I'm not going to show the newsmen.

MARYA: You told them you only have one pair of pants.

CHOPIN: I said pajamas. The translator said pants. I can't help that.

MARYA: Where are the socks?

CHOPIN: I'm wearing them.

MARYA: Take them off. I'll mend them.

CHOPIN: I'm not going to a ball. I'm going to prison.

MARYA: I'm ashamed. Please don't make me ashamed. I'm going to be here without you. The music in your hands will be too far away from me. I'll sit here silent, waiting. My keys unused.

CHOPIN: Let's practice my return. I'll walk in the door. We've forgotten how we smell. Maybe I'm wearing the socks. I've darned them in prison. I drop my bags. I run to you. I reach you—

*(Before* CHOPIN *can reach* MARYA, REAGAN *stops the scene.)*

REAGAN: Cut!

*(Blackout)*

*(The* REAGANS *consult.)*

REAGAN: Well, what do you think, Mommie?

BEEZO: I think they're wonderful.

REAGAN: So do I. Just the ones to play with the bear.

MARYA: The bear?

REAGAN: There's a bear, see, and there's a girl. The girl's being chased by the bear.

BEEZO: But you help her.

CHOPIN: How?

REAGAN: A piano appears. You come out. You see the bear.

BEEZO: You see the girl.

REAGAN: You want the girl.

CHOPIN: I want dignity for my people.

REAGAN: The bear growls. You edge over to your instrument, and you play wonderful music. The bear growls, and then it sits up and begins to sway in time to the music. Then, it actually starts dancing.

CHOPIN: Then what?

REAGAN: You get the girl.

BEEZO: And the piano.

CHOPIN: What if I stop playing?

REAGAN: What's that?

CHOPIN: When the dance is over, the bear is still a threat.

REAGAN: You get the...?

*(*BEEZO *helps him out.)*

REAGAN: I'll accept full responsibility.

BEEZO: You'll be a hero.

CHOPIN: I don't want to be a hero.

BEEZO: You'll be more than a hero. You'll be an international star. We'll put your hands in cement outside Graumann's Chinese Theater.

CHOPIN: Is this a bad dream?

REAGAN: Heck, no. It's the American Dream! Deal?

CHOPIN: Deal.

*(They shake hands.)*

CHOPIN: We're dead.

*(BEEZO encases CHOPIN's hands in cement.)*

BEEZO: Oh, no. You're immortal. Like Walter Brennan.

REAGAN: Come on, Mommie. We're going for a ride on a helicopter.

*(They exit. Blackout)*

MARYA: Look at you. Look at your hands.

CHOPIN: I'm immortal. Like Walter Brennan.

MARYA: You are not. Can you move your hands?

CHOPIN: Yes.

MARYA: Then Poland is not yet dead. This is some homecoming for you, Chopin.

CHOPIN: I'm home?

MARYA: Yes.

CHOPIN: What year is it?

MARYA: 1983.

CHOPIN: Danuta?

MARYA: What?

CHOPIN: Ah! Everything's clear. *(He exits and enters with a bouquet of flowers.)* My homecoming. I drop my bags. I run to you. I reach you. *(He dances MARYA around the room.)*

MARYA: There's no music.

CHOPIN: We have music. Just a minute. It's still here.

*(CHOPIN searches through his record collection. There is a knock at the door.)*

MARYA: I know what's going to happen. You're going to hold a news conference. Those newsmen are going to track mud all over my nice clean apartment. They laugh at our slip covers and make jokes about them in a foreign language.

*(Another knock at the door)*

MARYA: Go away! Every time there's a world crisis they hold it in my living room. You fill the room with flowers so people think we're happy. They know life in Poland isn't flowers. Show them how I make soup out of flowers after they leave. Show them that.

CHOPIN: We have to save Poland. They'll help us.

MARYA: Let someone else save Poland. Who's going to save us?

CHOPIN: Solidarity depends on me.

MARYA: Solidarity's been banned since you were in jail. Please, Chopin, can we sit as we used to, your head in my lap, and dream sweet dreams?

*(Another knock at the door)*

CHOPIN: That'll be the newsmen.

*(CHOPIN opens the door. STASH enters.)*

CHOPIN: Stash! Good old Stash!

*(STASH knocks CHOPIN to the ground.)*

CHOPIN: What the—Holy Father!

*(The POPE enters.)*

POPE: What is it, Lech?

CHOPIN: Ask Stash to let me up. He's breaking my neck.

POPE: Stash, this is the Holy Father speaking. Please let him up.

STASH: No.

POPE: Please, Stash.

STASH: He's a criminal parasite.

POPE: He's been to prison. Look here, Lech, you're in a very lucky position. He's not killing you.

CHOPIN: *(Coughing)* I can't breathe.

POPE: Stash, why don't you let him up? You want my Christmas blessing, don't you?

STASH: Holy Father, you're making a big deal out of nothing.

POPE: What's going to happen at Christmas, Stash, if the Christmas goose isn't blessed? Let him up.

*(STASH lets CHOPIN up.)*

STASH: Can I break something?

POPE: I wish you wouldn't.

*(STASH sees the records and begins smashing them, one by one.)*

CHOPIN: Stop! You're killing me!

STASH: It's for your own good. Would you rather the Russians do this? Be grateful you were visited by a countryman who knows what's best for you.

*(The* BEAR *enters.)*

STASH: Don't worry, it's under control.

*(The* BEAR *exits.)*

CHOPIN: Holy Father!

POPE: Being Polish is being patient, waiting for the right time. This is not the right time. Being Polish is knowing your limitations. Now Copernicus, he was a great Pole. He recognized that the earth was not the center of the universe. He was not the center of the universe. Get it? *(He starts.)* Wait a minute. This isn't... who got me to say that? Poland is the center of the universe. Poland is the Christ of Europe. We suffer. We die. We redeem Europe. The world follows the Poles. Copernicus was a heretic. *(He exits.)*

STASH: You'll thank me for this. *(Exits)*

CHOPIN: Are we not still alive?

MARYA: You were acquainting them with the circumstances of your death.

CHOPIN: No I wasn't. The Americans have a plan. Dream this dream with me.

MARYA: I'll dream I am your piano. You come to me. You unlock my keys. My music waits inside me for you to bring it out. You open me up.

*(Blackout)*

*(*MARYA *and* CHOPIN *as they were.)*

MARYA: You come to me. You sit beside me. You touch me and there is music. Your fingers dance on my keys. We sing for Poland.

*(They stare at each other. The* BEAR *enters.* CHOPIN *touches* MARYA. *A note. He touches her again. Another note. The* BEAR *approaches.* CHOPIN *plays* MARYA's *neck, her face, her arms. Lush, romantic music. The* BEAR *stops.* CHOPIN *plays* MARYA's *breasts, hips, thighs. Entranced, the* BEAR *paws* MARYA. MARYA *smacks the* BEAR *in the nose. The* BEAR *grabs* MARYA *and hauls her away.* CHOPIN *alone. Blackout)*

*(*CHOPIN *alone)*

CHOPIN: I will acquaint you with the known circumstances of my death. Two A M, the 17th of October, Place Vendome, Paris, France. 1849. With me is my sister Louise, other women. Teddy—you've seen his picture. Other women. No Marya. I lie on a day bed with a pillow at my head, my head thrown back to help me breathe. Teddy paints the pillow gold. My Adam's apple bulges, the vein over my right eye bulges, my lungs are full of fluid you can't see. My eyes squint, my ears are clotted, my lips slightly parted. They draw damp air. Teddy sketches my right side, my good side. I wear a soiled nightshirt. He makes it look clean. My fist is clenched. He omits it from the picture. My heart lives, beating time to a country full of music never heard, never to be heard. My heart yearns to beat in Poland. My body traps my heart. My body dies. I die. There is a post-mortem as per my request. No one remembers the result. There is a funeral. Mozart's Requiem is sung, as per my request. The church is full. The Requiem hasn't been heard since Napoleon was returned from St Helena. A loan of five thousand francs secures my burial. A small packet of earth from Poland secures my burial. And per my request, my heart is removed from my body and returned to Poland, to the Church of the Holy Cross. Where it still beats today. Where it beats for Poland.

*(Blackout)*

END OF PLAY

# NIXON APOLOGIZES TO THE NATION

# ORIGINAL PRODUCTION

NIXON APOLOGIZES TO THE NATION was first produced at the Wesleyan University Center for the Arts, opening on 4 March 1995. The cast and creative contributors were:

| | |
|---|---|
| SKIPPY | Simon Maclean |
| RICHARD M NIXON | Remy-Luc Auberjonois |
| EMILY DICKINSON | McKenna Kerrigan |
| DAN'L BOONE | Topher Bellavia |
| HARRIET BEECHER STOWE | Kayce L Davis |
| JOHNNY APPLESEED | Ben Boothby |
| BETSY ROSS | Stefanie Neuhauser |
| WALT WHITMAN | John Stuart Newman |
| GEORGE WASHINGTON | Kevin Hodes |
| MOM | Emma Ditrinco |
| J EDGAR HOOVER | Steven Myles Walsh |
| ANNOUNCER | Sean Connell |
| ANDY | Tony Field |
| KINGFISH & AMOS | Jeremy Goldstein |
| MAMA & NORTON | Janina Botchis |
| SAPPHIRE | Amanda L Bennett |
| ANNIE OAKLEY | Alix Lindsey Olson |
| DAN RATHER | Adam Hirsch |
| NIXON'S AIDES | Elijah Hawkes, Kenyon Phillips & William Ryan |
| *Director* | William H Francisco |
| *Dramaturg* | Gay Smith |
| *Set designer* | William R Ward |
| *Costume designer* | Leslie Weinberg |
| *Lighting designer* | John F Carr |
| *Sound consultant* | Mark Gawlak |

# CHARACTERS & SETTING

SKIPPY, *a presidential aide*
RICHARD M NIXON, *a president of the United States*
EMILY DICKINSON, *a first lady*
DAN'L BOONE, *a legend*
HARRIET BEECHER STOWE, *a paragon*
JOHNNY APPLESEED, *a visionary*
NIXON BABY, *the future*

BETSY ROSS, *a seamstress*
WALT WHITMAN, *a visionary*
GEORGE WASHINGTON, *the Father of His Country*
MOM, *a mom*

JEB MACGRUDER, *Presidential Advisor*
H R, *Presidential Advisor*
G GORDON LIDDY, *a real man*
J F K, *a real man in his own mind*
J EDGAR HOOVER, *a real man, but not in his own mind*

*A radio show cast:*
ANNOUNCER
ANDY
KINGFISH
AMOS,
MAMA
SAPPHIRE
NORTON

ANNIE OAKLEY, *a show woman*

DAN RATHER, *a poor successor to Walter Cronkite*

*Double, triple and quadruple casting urged*


*The action takes place in the Oval Office, the halls of the White House, and the United States of America.*


*The time is the not too distant and very distant past.*

# ACT ONE

*(The Oval Office)*

SKIPPY: The President Apologizes to the Nation. Take One. Three, two, one...

NIXON: My fellow Americans. The question on all our lips tonight is this: how the fuck did we get here?

SKIPPY: Cut!

NIXON: You know, once upon a time it wasn't like this...

SKIPPY: Mr President!

EMILY: *(Off)* Richard? Richard? Come to bed!

NIXON: Just a minute! I'm apologizing to the nation, for crying out loud!
   My fellow Americans: here we are, your embattled president, who did nothing wrong and only acted in the best interests of that nation, or any other nation, so conceived and so dedicated, and frankly speaking, I don't know how much longer your president can long endure.
   Your president needs your help, to look at our mutual heritage and see how we got to this moment of distrust, this moment where you don't even believe the man you elected to lead you, for Christ's sake!

SKIPPY: Mr President?

NIXON: Just a minute! We're going to have a look at everything that happened and get to the bottom of this. So, let's begin: I was born in humble circumstance.

*(The home of BETSY ROSS. BETSY and WALT WHITMAN sit sewing the flag.)*

BETSY: Delaware. Virginia...New Jersey...New York.

WALT: Pennsylvania...

BETSY: Pennsylvania...Rhode Island.

WALT: Massachusetts...Vermont. Maryland.

BETSY: Maryland.

WALT: North and South Carolina.

BETSY: North and South Carolina. How many is that?

WALT: Eleven.

BETSY: Didn't we count New York twice?

WALT: No.

BETSY: New Hampshire!

WALT: New Hampshire.

BETSY: There's how many more?

WALT: One.

BETSY: Wisconsin?

WALT: No.

BETSY: Montana?

WALT: Betsy Ross, what's gotten into you! It'll be years before they're states!

BETSY: Where will they go?

WALT: You just let some other seamstress worry about that. Thirteen is plenty.

BETSY: New Mexico?

WALT: Betsy! Where's your head these days? Betsy?

BETSY: Georgia?

WALT: Betsy Ross, look at me!

BETSY: What?

WALT: It doesn't matter what they're called, does it? As long as there are thirteen.

BETSY: No, Walt, I guess you're right. Should I put them in a circle? Or make a big "X"? Or leave the blue alone and put them on the stripes? I don't know.

WALT: Betsy?

BETSY: What?

WALT: Follow your heart. Although, they would look good on the blue.

BETSY: The blue.

WALT: Betsy? Is there something you want to tell me? Why don't I fix us a cup of coffee and you tell me all about it?

BETSY: Oh, Walt! Can't you see? I'm madly in love with that man!

WALT: Betsy, he's married.

BETSY: I don't care!

WALT: Have you told him?

BETSY: I can't. What if he laughs at me, or takes his flag to someone else? Oh, Walt, I feel terrible, burdening you when I know you'd rather be out writing poetry about presidents yet unborn. But you're my best friend; I have no one else. Helping me with the flag, sitting with me and being strong when he comes...

WALT: It's my country, too.

BETSY: Do you think he'd leave his wife for another?

WALT: The general has a lot on his mind these days. It's no small matter, running a country.

NIXON: That's for sure!

WALT: I'm afraid his personal happiness is second to the welfare of the country.

BETSY: Oh Walt, you don't know what it's like to love a man, yet never tell him. To work beside him, to feel his touch when he accidentally brushes my arm, reaching for the red stripes. You don't know what it's like when he talks about his men, to see the passion in his eyes and wonder if somehow, some way—

WALT: That passion might be for you?

BETSY: You asked what was in my heart and I told you!

WALT: Perhaps, if you feel this strongly, you should say something.

BETSY: Oh, Walt, I couldn't. I can only tell you.

WALT: Yet this unspoken love wants to shout its name, no matter the consequences.

BETSY: Yes, oh yes! Walt, will you speak for me?

WALT: What?

BETSY: You're my best friend. You know the General. You have a way with words. When he comes, could you speak for me?

WALT: I can't know your heart, Betsy, any more than you could know mine.

BETSY: But Walt, while you have not my ardor, I have not your art. Surely, you can tell him that I tremble at the thought of his touch, and if he deigned to hear my plea, I would return his love one hundred times for every star I sewed.

WALT: Surely you can tell him yourself.

BETSY: I ask you as a friend, Walt. Please speak to him of my passion that knows not its voice.

WALT: *(Aside)* If only she knew of the love that dares not speak its name within mine own breast for this same father of our country; how only our friendship, and her speaking first, prevented me this day from making my passions known. How I took up sewing, and pricked my finger countless times seven when I thought I heard his carriage go by.

But she's Betsy Ross, and I am just a poet. Her love, while unspeakable, is less so than mine.

NIXON: You can't trust him, Betsy! Don't do it. He's a liberal!

WALT: I'll speak with the General.

NIXON: Oh, rats!

*(Clop-clop-clop of a horse outside)*

BETSY: That's his horse now! Oh, Walt, thank you so much! I was afraid that you thought maybe I was leading you on.

WALT: Oh, no!

BETSY: Oh, yes! I never considered your feelings, only mine own!
But here he comes!
I'll wait behind this screen! No, in the closet! No, behind the screen. And if your very best efforts fail, I shall fling myself from this window, which is also behind this screen, to a cobblestone death, for I can no longer live without his love.

WALT: What should I tell him about the stars? Do you have a fallback pattern? Betsy!

*(A knock at the door)*

BETSY: He's here! Good luck, Walt! *(She hides.)*

*(The Oval Office. EMILY appears in a nightgown.)*

EMILY: I rose to your requirement, dropped the playthings of my life to take the honorable work of woman and of wife.

NIXON: That's fine, dear, but you're not needed. Go back to bed.

EMILY: I rose to your requirement....

NIXON: I know, I know. I'll call you if I need you.

*(She disappears.)*

NIXON: You know my wife. Writes poetry up in the attic. A good woman. Some would say she's too good for me, that my daughters are too good for me. But I came by them all honestly, there was no subterfuge or chicanery. MacGruder can vouch for that. Jeb? Can you vouch for your president, that his wife and daughters love him? Where's Jeb MacGruder?

SKIPPY: Jeb's not here, Sir. It's Skippy.

NIXON: Where were we?

SKIPPY: I think it was your parents, Sir.

NIXON: That's right! How we got here...

(WALT WHITMAN *lies in bed.* GEORGE WASHINGTON *gets dressed.*)

WALT: What do you think about when we make love?

GEORGE: After?

WALT: During. When we make love.

GEORGE: I don't know. I can't say exactly.

WALT: Don't know? Or won't say?

GEORGE: I think of flowers. Birds. I think about the country. My men. Why we fight, what it'll be like when it's over. How you're coming with the flag.

WALT: You think of me?

GEORGE: Of course!

WALT: How do you think of me?

GEORGE: Kinda warm. And soft. What's the problem?

WALT: Nothing.

GEORGE: Nothing! I know it's something.

WALT: You don't think about those things.

GEORGE: What do I think about?

WALT: I don't know. You seem so distant.

NIXON: He's the president, for cripe's sakes!

GEORGE: A man's got to be free, he can't be tied down, Walt. I mean, Life! Liberty!

WALT: Happiness?

GEORGE: You can pursue happiness. No guarantees.

WALT: Are you happy?

GEORGE: I'm pursuing happiness.

WALT: Oh. And that's what you think about when we make love?

GEORGE: I've got to get back to Valley Forge. You'll say nothing of this to Betsy. Walt? You won't mention this to Betsy?

WALT: I won't say anything.

GEORGE: Hey! What's the matter?

WALT: Nothing.

GEORGE: Hey, Walt! Stop by the camp: the troops love when you bring those chocolates and blankets. You're good for morale!

WALT: Yeah.

GEORGE: I mean it.

WALT: I mean, what about me, what about us? Why is it that saving the country is more important than what just happened? You could be a great man, right here!

GEORGE: I think you're a great guy.

WALT: Yeah.

GEORGE: Gotta go. Walt? Walter?

WALT: What?

GEORGE: I gotta go.

WALT: So go!

GEORGE: What are you going to do?

WALT: I'll probably write something.

GEORGE: Hah-hah. Not about this. Walt? I have enough to explain. Walt?

WALT: Goodbye!

GEORGE: Gotta go!

WALT: George?

GEORGE: What?

WALT: Goodbye.

*(Blackout)*

*(The Oval Office)*

SKIPPY: The President Apologizes to the Nation...take Two.

NIXON: Goodbye, Walt.

SKIPPY: Walt, Sir? There's no one on the appointment list by that name, Sir. It's MacGruder at ten, Haldeman and Erlichmann at eleven.

NIXON: My mother was a saint, did you know that, Skippy?

SKIPPY: Sir?

NIXON: You go back, you see the sacrifices people made, how we got here.

SKIPPY: Did you want to try that speech again?

NIXON: There were great men before me. And great women, too! And the liberals!

*(Fade out)*

*(BETSY's house. She is sewing. There is a knock at the door.)*

BETSY: Is that you, General?

*(WALT enters.)*

WALT: It's me Betsy. Walt. Walt Whitman.

BETSY: Oh, Walt. Did you speak with the General?

WALT: I did.

BETSY: What did he say? No, first tell me what you said.

WALT: About...?

BETSY: You know what about!

WALT: We talked about you. And the flag. He said he didn't much mind what arrangement, because he expected new—

BETSY: Did you tell him I dropped everything to work on this flag, because I'm crazy for his love, people say it's this hot weather, but it's him, and only him!

WALT: Betsy? Betsy? Listen to me: I'm going to have a baby.

NIXON: The little bastard!

BETSY: Oh, Walt! That's wonderful, if that's what you want! I'm so happy for you! I didn't—but what does this have to do with me and the General?

WALT: Betsy, I think we should sit down.

BETSY: Of course, how silly of me! I mean, if you're going to have a baby, you should sit down. You see how distraught I've been, only thinking of myself. Let me fix you something, some tea, or coffee, or a glass of milk; maybe some fruit—

WALT: I'm going to have the General's baby.
   Betsy?

BETSY: My General?

WALT: Yes.

*(She throws down the flag and stomps on it.)*

WALT: Betsy, what are you doing!

BETSY: I'm going to burn it. I'm going to burn his flag and to the republic for which it stands!

NIXON: Look what he's made her do!

WALT: Betsy! Please! Get hold! Listen to yourself! Betsy!

BETSY: I trusted you! How could you do this to me!

WALT: It was easy, Betsy, it was glorious, the best sex I ever had! Bold! Hilarious! We wept for love and joy! At first I felt guilty, but then, what did it matter? I was helpless in his arms, endlessly rocking! Sure, I betrayed you, if you want the truth, but when he looked in my eyes, every thought of you and my good intentions went out the window.

NIXON: Wouldn't you think a little white lie would've been better here?

WALT: He left me in the end, but I knew he'd left something of himself within me!

BETSY: He left you?

WALT: Yes, Betsy, he did. But don't confuse the man with the country he fights to create. Burn not our flag, but wash it, and may it blow dry forever in the wind. And Betsy?

BETSY: What?

WALT: Excuse me... *(He gives birth, handing the baby to* BETSY.*)* Now that you know the truth, raise this love child as your own.

BETSY: Walt?!?

WALT: Goodbye, Betsy, and thanks! *(He exits.)*

BABY: Whaaaaaaaaa!

*(*BETSY *cradles the baby, humming it a lullaby.)*

BETSY: Are you going to grow up to be a warrior like your daddy, or an artist like your daddy?

BABY: I'm going to be president, from sea to shining sea.

BETSY: Oh, that's a lot for a little baby!

NIXON: I'll work hard, Mommie. Honest.

BETSY: You have to work like a dog, Richard. Can you do that for your Mommie?

*(*NIXON *pants.)*

BETSY: Good boy! Now, sit up and beg!

*(*NIXON *begs.)*

BETSY: What are you begging for?

NIXON: I want to be president!

BETSY: For approval! You're begging for approval. Because you're not my favorite! Good doggie! Now, roll over.

*(*NIXON *rolls over.)*

(BETSY *hits him on the nose.*)

BETSY: What are you doing?

NIXON: You told me to roll over!

BETSY: Never roll over for anyone. Not anyone! Now, sit up! Sit up straight! It's alright, you can do it.

(NIXON *sits up.*)

BETSY: Good, good!

(SKIPPY *enters.*)

SKIPPY: Mr President, Sir?

NIXON: Can't it wait? I'm just a little puppy, for Chrissakes!

SKIPPY: Should I stop taping, Sir?

NIXON: What?

BETSY: Now I want you to put on your best clothes, go to your one-room schoolhouse, and learn how hard and cruel life is.

NIXON: Yes, Mommie.

SKIPPY: Would that be, Yes, Mommie, stop taping, or Yes, Mommie, let it roll, Sir?

NIXON: I can explain everything! Roll the tape!

(*Blackout*)

(*The Oval Office*)

SKIPPY: The President Apologizes to the Nation...take Three.

NIXON: My fellow Americans. Lincoln wasn't the only one who began humbly. Your president was a bright and eager lad in the school of hard knocks. Adversity was my university. Out on the frontier. Where danger lurked, I was trying to get an education.

(*The scene shifts to a log cabin.*)

(DAN'L BOONE *points a rifle out the window.*)

(JEB MACGRUDER *plays harmonica.* HARRIET *teaches* NIXON *his A B Cs.*)

NIXON: Do you want to hear my A B Cs? (*He recites them.*)

HARRIET: Oh, Dan'l, Dan'l, please come away from that window.

DAN'L: Skippy, put that mouth organ away!

JEB: Mouth organ sets a mood, boss. Whatcha aiming at?

DAN'L: Apple grower out there. Planting apple seeds. And you, shut yer yap!

NIXON: Now that I've done my A B Cs, tell me what you think of me!

DAN'L: I thought I told you to shut it! *(He kicks NIXON.)*

NIXON: Ow!

DAN'L: I hurt you, poochie?

NIXON: Yeah.

DAN'L: Well, shut yer yap unless I ask you something, or I'll hurt you again. You gonna be a dog all your life?

HARRIET: He can't be president without learning his A B Cs!

DAN'L: Other things to learn around here besides that! Like taking it like a man!

NIXON: What about dishing it out?

DAN'L: First you'll learn to take it! Damn apple growers! Spreading their seed everywhere, indiscriminate! Soon the whole damn country be overrun by free apples. Where does that leave us? Honest business man trying to sell oranges!

HARRIET: What do you think, Richard? Are apples better than oranges? Or the other way around?

NIXON: I'm prepared to argue either way. What does he think?

HARRIET: Richard! You should take a stand.

NIXON: Oh, alright. On what?

HARRIET: You've got a lot to learn. Have you read my book, *Uncle Tom's Cabin*?

NIXON: No.

DAN'L: That's commie poop!

HARRIET: It is not! It calls for the abolition of slavery, and you know what Mr Lincoln said when he met me.

NIXON: What?

DAN'L: You're the little woman who started this big war! B F D, Harriet! I got apple men in my orange grove and you want more people running around free.

HARRIET: Ignore him, Richard. If you're going to be president, you should know about the black man, how he's suffered.

NIXON: If that's what it takes, I'll do it.

JOHNNY: *(Singing, offstage)* Fal-de-ri, fal de ra...

*(DAN'L fires.)*

DAN'L: Got him! Now go fetch!

(JEB *exits.*)

DAN'L: Want to know what I think?

NIXON: I'm all ears!

DAN'L: Stop them at the borders. And where you see them, cut them down, root them out! You're a good little pooch!

NIXON: Don't hit me!

DAN'L: I ain't gonna hit you! Friendly cuff on the ear. You can take it.

(DAN'L *cuffs* NIXON.)

NIXON: *(Aside)* I'll get even some day.

DAN'L: I heard that! You and what army!

NIXON: Just kidding! A dog never forgets.

HARRIET: That's an elephant, Richard.

NIXON: I'll be an elephant with a little bit of dog!

HARRIET: You can be anything you want!

(JEB *carries* JOHNNY *into the cabin.*)

SKIPPY: Here's your apple guy.

DAN'L: Check his I D.

(JEB *checks his I D.*)

DAN'L: His own damn fault! He was on my land!

SKIPPY: Driver's license says Johnny Appleseed. You killed Johnny Appleseed.

HARRIET: Johnny Appleseed!

JEB: We're in trouble, boss! This guy is a minor folk legend. What are we going to do?

NIXON: It wasn't his fault!

JEB: Was, too!

DAN'L: Was not! Was it?

NIXON: You've got to take the fall on this one, Jeb. I'll need you later.

JEB: Me! Why me!

NIXON: Because you're expendable. He was protecting you. And the woman!

DAN'L: Nixon, you little son of a bitch, you're my kind of dog!

JEB: Protecting us from Johnny Appleseed?

HARRIET: He's coming to!

(JOHNNY *revives*.)

DAN'L: Damn liberals! What's it take to shut them down! What was you doing on my land?

JOHNNY: I have a vision for this country of ours: I plant apple trees, so people can share the fruit and live in harmony. Nobody has to starve in my America. If you're hungry, have an apple! Poor person goes by, wants an apple, go on and take it! Maybe kids grab a rotten apple, toss it back and forth harmlessly and invent baseball! A kid can dream of pitching the last out of the World Series. Bases loaded, full count, the windup, the pitch, the runners going—and radio! Picture a nation of people, as big and generous as this land, bonded by baseball, fellowship and my apples!

DAN'L: We're football around these parts.

JOHNNY: No reason to shoot a fella, just because he disagrees with you.

NIXON: He didn't do it. There's your man: MacGruder!

JEB: What?

DAN'L: Jeb, apologize to the man!

NIXON: Wait. It was an honest mistake. No reason to apologize.

JOHNNY: Beg your pardon, but I think there is. I'd like an apology, then I'll dust myself off and be on my way.

DAN'L: He wants an apology! Get him, Nixon!

NIXON: I'll make you a little deal: you'll get your apology if I could have one of those radios you were talking about.

JOHNNY: You got yourself a deal.

NIXON: Well?

JEB: Sorry I shot you.

JOHNNY: Forgive and forget, that's my motto.

NIXON: (Little twerp!) So, where is it? The radio.

JOHNNY: You'll get it, I promise. So: Guess I'll be on my way.

DAN'L: Here's your coat, what's your hurry?

JOHNNY: Wait. For the lady of the house. (*He gives her an apple.*)

HARRIET: Thank you, Johnny Appleseed!

(*He exits.*)

DAN'L: He's spreading free apples all over the country. What are you going to do about it?

HARRIET: There's nothing un-American about apples, Dan'l.

NIXON: Rotten apples?

SKIPPY: Mr President? Want to try again? Mr President?

DAN'L: Mr President? That guy's a menace. Soon he's going to have apples in every home in America. Red apples!

NIXON: I want you to do me a favor. Get me a hatchet.

DAN'L: Consider it done.

*(He exits. The sound of broken glass. He returns with a hatchet and hands it to NIXON.)*

NIXON: Good, good! Now, I want you to follow him. Find out where he goes, what he does.

DAN'L: It won't be pretty.

NIXON: And get me some dirt!

DAN'L: Yes, Sir!

NIXON: And if you get caught—

DAN'L: I don't get caught, Sir. But if I did...

NIXON: What?

DAN'L: Dead men tell no tales.

NIXON: They can't kick you around.

DAN'L: They can't kick you around, either, Sir! *(He exits.)*

*(The Oval Office)*

SKIPPY: Mr President? Want to try the apology again? Sir?

NIXON: They can't kick Nixon around any more?

SKIPPY: The President Apologizes to the Nation...take Four.

NIXON: Wait a minute!

SKIPPY: The camera's rolling, Sir!

*(NIXON goes looking for the apple tree. He chops it down.)*

*(MOM enters.)*

MOM: Richard? Richard?

NIXON: Damn! It's my mother!

MOM: Oh! Look at your father's tree! Someone chopped it down! The poor little cherry tree!

NIXON: *(Aside)* Cherry tree?

MOM: His beautiful tree! Why did they chop it down?

NIXON: You said cherry tree? *(Aside)* I've got a way out!

MOM: Who did this?

NIXON: I didn't chop any cherry tree down. Honest!

MOM: Oh, Richard, I didn't accuse you—what is that behind your back?

NIXON: Where?

MOM: Behind your back.

NIXON: Nothing.

MOM: Where did you get that hatchet?

NIXON: What hatchet?

MOM: This hatchet!

NIXON: Some men.

MOM: Did you chop this tree down?

NIXON: This cherry tree?

MOM: You know what I mean! This tree!

NIXON: I chopped down no cherry trees.

MOM: Richard: look me in the eye when I ask you. Did you chop down your father's cherry tree with this hatchet?

NIXON: No.

*(She embraces him.)*

MOM: Oh, Richard, I wish I could believe you!

NIXON: You can, Mommie!

*(She exits.)*

NIXON: Skippy! Where are you?

*(SKIPPY enters.)*

SKIPPY: Yes, Sir?

NIXON: Get rid of this hatchet.

SKIPPY: What should I do with it?

NIXON: I don't care. Just get rid of it!

SKIPPY: Are you ready for your speech, Sir? To the nation?

NIXON: I could make a speech now, yes. I could admit I chopped the damned tree down.

SKIPPY: Yes, Sir.

NIXON: I'm not the first, Skippy.

SKIPPY: Sir?

NIXON: To tell a little white lie. To save the nation.

SKIPPY: No, Sir.

NIXON: But would they understand?

SKIPPY: Could you put it to them, Sir, and let them make up their own minds?

NIXON: Don't be naive. The Father of His Country. He was no saint.

SKIPPY: Sir?

NIXON: I told you to get rid of that hatchet.

SKIPPY: Yes, Sir.

NIXON: I have things on him. Not that I'd use them. No, Sir. I'm bigger than that. Unless I have to.
Get rid of the hatchet. I never saw the damn thing!

SKIPPY: Yes, Sir. *(He gets rid of the hatchet.)*

NIXON: He was no saint.

*(Blackout)*

*(The Oval Office)*

SKIPPY: The President Apologizes to the Nation...take Five.

NIXON: Wait a minute. Could we begin again?

SKIPPY: The President Apologizes to the Nation...take Six...

NIXON: Good evening, my fellow Americans. Then there were the war years. I was in the South Pacific—

SKIPPY: Mr President?

NIXON: —running a little trading post on a small island. Not much in the way of entertainment back there. If I could only get my hands on a radio.

*(J F K enters with a radio.)*

J F K: Hey! You "Nick" Nixon?

NIXON: I hate that nickname! Who wants to know?

J F K: Jack Kennedy. My P T boat just got rammed by a Jap supply ship. Had to swim ashore. What do you do for kicks around here?

NIXON: You swam here? That's thirteen miles!

J F K: It was nothing. Say, I heard you're about the best fellow in the Pacific if a guy needs a favor.

NIXON: What do you need?

J F K: A bottle of gin, a pretty girl, and a story for the voters.

NIXON: Voters? Story?

J F K: Can't tell them the truth! Lost my boat, half my crew. Not quite the war story to get me to the White House!

NIXON: You swam to shore! And you're going to the White House? So am I! Is that a radio? Because *Amos 'n Andy*'s on. F D R's favorite show. I love Amos 'n Andy!

J F K: You want it? Be my guest. (*He gives* NIXON *the radio.*)

NIXON: Oh, boy! Thanks! What do you want back?

J F K: Don't worry about it.

NIXON: I've got some bourbon. Maybe we could listen to *Amos 'n Andy* and talk politics?

J F K: No, thanks. I think we can do better!

NIXON: I like them. Where are you going?

J F K: Swim back to where the action is. Want to come?

NIXON: I can't sw—no, thanks. But thanks for the radio!

J F K: Share and share alike! (*He exits.*)

NIXON: Don't you want to be my friend? Bye, Jack!

SKIPPY: CUT!!!

NIXON: It's F D R's favorite show, for crying out loud!

SKIPPY: Sir?

NIXON: *Amos 'n Andy!*

SKIPPY: I don't recall, Sir. If you want to keep the camera rolling—

(NIXON *takes a mighty swig of bourbon.*)

NIXON: Is that thing loaded? I don't want any tape! F D R: he knew radio!

SKIPPY: Before my time, Sir. Hold the cameras...

NIXON: He used to sit here and talk on the radio. Like I'm doing here, behind a desk like mine, in his wheelchair, pretending he wasn't crippled, the presidency was whole and intact, and so was the President.... Sat here like me, savoring a drink with the air conditioning full blast, a fire roaring in the hearth, maybe some Mantovanni in the background—I heard he broadcast in his underwear sometimes. Who knew?

SKIPPY: No one, Sir.

NIXON: They re-elected him three times! In his underwear! Kennedy's father bought him an election. I was an obscure congressman from Whittier, trying to save the country from the Reds, and the president was in his underwear!

SKIPPY: I don't think they had Mantovanni, Sir.

NIXON: What's that?

SKIPPY: Before his time.

NIXON: What did they have?

SKIPPY: Couldn't say, Sir.

NIXON: He had *Amos 'n Andy*, that's what he had! How else can you tell what the colored people were thinking?

SKIPPY: Sir, they weren't—

NIXON: Don't interrupt!

SKIPPY: Yes, Sir.

NIXON: And this is his old radio, the one he used to listen to. So let's just turn it on.

SKIPPY: I don't know if we can—

NIXON: I'm the chief executive!

(NIXON *turns on the radio.*)

ANNOUNCER: And now for *The Amos 'n Andy Show,* brought to you by the Committee to Elect Dick Nixon Senator!

(*The radio show begins, as if in the radio studio.*)

ANDY: Let me get this straight, Kingfish, before we set out for Ebbets Field to see Jackie Robinson play: you going to make this year's Mystic Knights of the Sea Fish Fry the biggest of all time, so big you're going to invite Jackie Robinson himself?

KINGFISH: That's right, Andy.

ANDY: Was it the dues we collected?

KINGFISH: No, sir.

ANDY: Was it the raffle we ran?

KINGFISH: You know it wasn't the raffle.

ANDY: Was it from money left over from last year?

KINGFISH: No, Sir.

ANDY: Was it the raffle we ran?

KINGFISH: You know it wan't the raffle.

ANDY: Was it from money left over from last year?

KINGFISH: Now Andy, you know we been losing money year after year, hambone over fist.

ANDY: So how are we going to finance the Fry and get Jackie Robinson to make an appearance?

*(Sound effects of a door opening, and* SAPPHIRE *appears.)*

SAPPHIRE: George Stevens, have you been prowling around my boudoir?

KINGFISH: Why no, honey pie, I ain't been in the boudoir since you booted me out.

SAPPHIRE: Don't you sweet talk me, George Stevens. You know that the most valuable item in my boudoir is the tape of Mr Abraham Lincoln getting shot in Ford's Theatre by my great-granddaddy.

KINGFISH: Honey, I didn't even know you had the tape.

SAPPHIRE: I can't find it, George. It was tucked securely under my corsets.

KINGFISH: Honey, I swear to you on a stack of Bibles, ain't nothing ever gets out from under your corsets.

SAPPHIRE: Here it is! All I can say, George, is that it's a good thing it's still in this box. Mama and I are giving it to the Reverend, for safe keeping!

*(SFX car horn outside.)*

SAPPHIRE: That's Mama now, in Amos' cab.

KINGFISH: Why Sapphire, I could take that tape and do something harmful with it. But it would be wrong! That tape could cause a lot of problems if it falls into the wrong hands.

SAPPHIRE: That's right, George.

NIXON: It would be wrong!

*(SFX car horn.)*

SAPPHIRE: Mama hates to wait. Good day to you, Andy. Enjoy yourself at Ebbets Field.

ANDY: Thanks, Mrs Stevens. When Jackie Robinson gets up to the plate, I'll give an extra cheer for you.

SAPPHIRE: I'd like that. COMING, MAMA! *(She exits.)*

*(SFX door closes.)*

ANDY: Kingfish, for a minute I thought you swiped the one thing that could undo the colored folk for all time.

KINGFISH: Hah! I pulled The Great Switcheroonie! She got the poke, and I got the pig. I'm meeting a reporter at the Lodge right now. And if he agrees it's authentic, we got the do-re-mi to get Jackie Robinson to the Fry.

ANDY: But Kingfish, what are people going to think when they see your wife's great-granddaddy shoot the one president that treated our people decent?

(EMILY DICKINSON *and* MOM *enter.*)

MOM: Richard?

(NIXON *turns off the radio.*)

NIXON: Yes, Mother?

EMILY: Richard?

NIXON: Pat! Have you been drinking?

EMILY: Wild Nights—Wild Nights!

MOM: Have you finished your homework?

NIXON: Yes, Mother.

MOM: Then don't you think it's time for bed?

EMILY: Were I with thee
Wild Night should be
Our luxury!

NIXON: That's enough. I'm very busy. Oh, Mother, can I just stay up a little while longer?

MOM: Now Richard, tomorrow is Halloween, you know you'll be out late looking for Communists, and I want you to get a good night's sleep.

NIXON: But Mommie, how am I going to be president, if I have to—did you say Communists?

EMILY: Futile—the Winds—
To a Heart in port—
Done with the Compass—
Done with the Chart!

NIXON: I'm working on the campaign. What if the Communists come and get me?

MOM: Do I get a kiss? Richard?

EMILY: Rowing in Eden—
Ah, the Sea!
Might I but moor—Tonight—
In Thee!

NIXON: If I give you a kiss, can I stay up?

MOM: I think you should just kiss me goodnight.

NIXON: Two kisses and I stay up.

(*He kisses his* MOM. *She exits.*)

NIXON: I'm going to be president some day.

EMILY: Might I but moor—Tonight—
In Thee?

NIXON: I'll go when I'm damned well ready!

(*She exits.*)

(SKIPPY *enters.*)

SKIPPY: Mr President? Are we ready? Mr President?

NIXON: I've got to find those Commies, for Chrissakes! Get Liddy in here!

SKIPPY: Yes, Sir.

(LIDDY *enters.*)

NIXON: What've you got?

LIDDY: I followed the little Red to California; there was apples everywhere. Red apples.

NIXON: How do you like that!

LIDDY: Then the trail got cold; I was out in the desert. All alone. The desert was cold, so cold I had to light my hand to keep warm.

NIXON: Wow.

LIDDY: Then this woman comes along.

NIXON: Who?

LIDDY: Who! The one you're running against for Senate.
There I was, out in the desert.

(*The desert*)

(ANNIE OAKLEY *enters on horseback.*)

LIDDY: Who the fuck are you?

ANNIE: I'm Annie Oakley. I can outshoot any man, outride any Injun, and outlove any woman in the West. Come here, stranger.

(*She kisses* LIDDY *all over.*)

LIDDY: Stop it! Yuck! Get away from me! Let go!

ANNIE: I was offering you unconditional love, friend.

LIDDY: You got a funny way of showing it!

ANNIE: You want to be in my act? I'm running for Senate: Straight Shooting Annie Oakley versus Tricky Dick Nixon. It's a wonderful act!

LIDDY: How straight do you shoot?

ANNIE: Put an apple on your head.

LIDDY: Yeah?

ANNIE: And I'll cut it in two.

LIDDY: Sounds intriguing.

ANNIE: Wanna be part of my team?

LIDDY: Love to. Tell me everything.

ANNIE: I like you, stranger. I like all strangers, but I like you especial. This here's my husband. Melvyn Douglas, the actor.

(JOHNNY APPLESEED enters.)

LIDDY: It was him, Sir! With your opponent!

NIXON: How do you like that!

LIDDY: What kind of name is Douglas?

ANNIE: Show biz name!

LIDDY: Do you know her husband's real name is Melvyn Hesselberg?

ANNIE: Given the climate, friend, it's not a name that sells tickets, exactly.

LIDDY: I got some other stuff on her, too.

NIXON: Start working the phones: the voters have got to know.

(The Oval Office)

SKIPPY: The President Apologizes to the Nation. Take Seven.

NIXON: I'm trying to explain my race for Senator from the great state of California—I wouldn't say this publicly—against a woman who's pink down to her underwear, an advocate of unconditional, free love who travels with known Communists, whose husband, I didn't say this but I heard it, has a Jewish name: what's she afraid of and why doesn't she use it?

SKIPPY: You can't start that way, Sir.

NIXON: I didn't say that!

SKIPPY: Could we stop it there?

LIDDY: We'll get on it, Sir! May I say I'm proud to serve the office you hold?

NIXON: Just keep your hand out of the fire and on the phone!

*(LIDDY exits.)*

*(ANNIE enters.)*

ANNIE: Mr President, I need—what are you doing here? I come looking for Mr Truman and find you!

NIXON: I would never suggest you're looking for Mr Truman because Mrs Truman is out of town.

ANNIE: Hey, friend, I don't like the way you're slinging mud.

NIXON: Me?

ANNIE: I see posters all over saying I don't shoot straight.

NIXON: I don't know anything about it.

ANNIE: Of all the low-down, low level skunks I seen in this business, you're the worst. You're so low, you got to go tip-toe to kiss the backside of a rattlesnake!

NIXON: Sticks and stones!

ANNIE: Call off your dogs, Nixon, and fight fair!

NIXON: Woof, woof. Why don't we just let the voters decide?

*(ANNIE disappears.)*

*(Blackout)*

*(The Oval Office. NIXON lies asleep at his desk.)*

SKIPPY: Mr President? Sir, are you asleep?

*(NIXON wakes up suddenly.)*

NIXON: What's that? No! Never asleep! I was listening. Did you hear?

SKIPPY: No, Sir.

NIXON: I was listening for my wife. Upstairs. She's up there.

SKIPPY: Would you like some coffee, Mr President?

NIXON: She's kinda quiet. Some would say a recluse. But she can help me. The kids can help me. I have a wonderful family.

SKIPPY: Yes, Sir.

NIXON: Maybe if people realized I wasn't such a bad guy, what do you say? If they knew that I bleed, too, fall in love, go ouch when I bump into things? I used to go out on Halloween. That's how I met Mrs Nixon.

SKIPPY: I'll get you some coffee, Sir. *(Exits)*

*(NIXON puts on his Uncle Sam costume.)*

(J F K *and* HOOVER *enter in costume.* J F K *as a P T Commander,* HOOVER *in a dress.*)

J F K: Hey, Nick! We're trick or treating. Want to join us? Where did you get that goofy costume?

NIXON: I made this costume with my mother's help. She sewed some of it, but I sewed the rest.

J F K: Won't get many pretty women with that.

HOOVER: He's not looking for women. He's looking for Communists.

J F K: Tonight's Halloween!

HOOVER: The best time!

NIXON: How do I look, Mother? I'm all dressed up! How do I look?

(MOM *appears.*)

MOM: Let me fix you, darling. Tuck in your shirt.

NIXON: But Mother, I sewed these stars on myself. And if people don't see them, they won't know how hard I worked on my costume.

MOM: They don't have to. They'll see a good and decent young boy dressed like Uncle Sam! Aren't you going to introduce me to your friends?

NIXON: No.

MOM: Very well. Now you run along and enjoy yourself! (*She exits.*)

J F K: Hey, Nick, there's a sorority house over here! Let's hit it up!

HOOVER: You're looking for Reds!

NIXON: House to house, looking for Reds. I especially liked the dark houses, where you could maybe see a light on in the back, maybe the blue flicker of a television set.

HOOVER: You've got to go where other children dare not go.

NIXON: But I'd go.

HOOVER: Just go up there, never mind if the porch light was off, don't slip on the wet leaves on the steps.

NIXON: Like this?

J F K: Oh, Nick!

HOOVER: Ring the doorbell. Wait a while.

NIXON: There's no one here.

HOOVER: Ring it again. Listen for footsteps sneaking to the basement.

J F K: Come on, Nick!

HOOVER: Knock, very loud, in case the doorbell didn't work.

NIXON: Anybody home? *(He knocks.)*

HOOVER: Yell it out, in case they didn't hear you knock, or didn't think you were serious.

NIXON: Trick or treat! *(He knocks.)*

J F K: Nick, those girls won't wait forever!

HOOVER: Take a good look around. If there's more than a day of mail in the mail box—put your finger through the slot and poke around—maybe they're really not there.

NIXON: Maybe they did go out on the one night of the year everyone else stays home to give a hard-working kid like me candy and maybe a shiny new Lincoln penny.

HOOVER: But they have to come back some time. Wait them out. Look around.

NIXON: Could I visit another house where ghosts and goblins come and go?

HOOVER: But that would be the easy way.

NIXON: The easy way.

J F K: See you later, Nick. I'm getting laid.

NIXON: No! Jack! We can do this together! Jack? Won't you be my friend?

HOOVER: Get on with it!

*(NIXON knocks again.)*

NIXON: The third time is usually—

*(EMILY appears at the door.)*

EMILY: What do you want from me!

NIXON: Trick or treat!

J F K: Bingo!

EMILY: Oh, you're that pathetic little boy from down the street.

NIXON: Do you have anything for me?

EMILY: No.

NIXON: Are you sure?

EMILY: Yes, I'm sure!

HOOVER: Ask about the Reds!

NIXON: Can I look around?

EMILY: No, you can't. Could you please leave? I'm very busy.

NIXON: In the kitchen, cellar? Under the bed?

J F K: Go, Nick!

EMILY: Look, if you're trying to sell anything I've got a big dog. And my brother should be home any minute.

NIXON: Okay, okay. But could I have a trick or treat?

EMILY: I don't have anything.

NIXON: Could you look?

EMILY: Oh, very well. But wait here. *(She vanishes.)*

NIXON: This one is a recluse who writes strange poetry and won't show it to anyone. I think she can be trusted.

HOOVER: Yeah.

J F K: Yep.

*(EMILY returns with an apple.)*

EMILY: Here.

NIXON: Is this all? No candy, no shiny Lincoln pennies?

EMILY: It's all I have.

J F K: Don't give up!

NIXON: I don't like apples. But I'll take it for my sickly brother, who can't go from door to door because of his condition. You don't have anything else?

EMILY: Please! I'm very busy! Would you kindly leave?

HOOVER: Get the goods!

NIXON: What about one of those poems you've got upstairs in your bedroom? The ones you've been working on when you think no one is watching? About not stopping for death and making it stop for you, or being nobody, and wondering if I'm nobody, too!

J F K: Oh, Nick, you dog!

EMILY: Get out of my house!

NIXON: But you see, I'm not nobody. I'm Uncle Sam. You wouldn't have another apple?

*(She slams the door in his face.)*

HOOVER: Let's go.

J F K: No, Nick, it's love at first sight!

NIXON: Really?

J F K: She likes you!

NIXON: She does like me! If she was that threatened, maybe I can trust her.

J F K: Give her a go!

*(He knocks on the door.)*

NIXON: Hello? Hello?

*(*SKIPPY *appears.)*

SKIPPY: Mr President? Mr President? We're ready with the equipment, if you are, Sir.

NIXON: Not now! I'm proposing! *(He knocks at the door.)*

SKIPPY: The crew is ready, Sir, should I send them away?

NIXON: Yes! Send them away!

SKIPPY: Okay, everybody, let's take lunch!

J F K: Nick, you want me to do this for you?

NIXON: No! There's some things a man's got to take personal responsibility for! Wait on the side, don't let her see you.

J F K: Okay, sport!

HOOVER: I can't stop for love, Nixon. *(He exits.)*

*(*NIXON *knocks at the door.)*

*(*EMILY *answers.)*

EMILY: What do you want!

NIXON: Will you marry me?

J F K: Oh, Nick!

NIXON: Not now, but later?

EMILY: No! You're a horrible person!

*(She slams the door, but* NIXON's *foot stops it.)*

EMILY: Look. I'm trying to write a poem. You've interrupted my concentration with your knocking and your rude chatter and all this nonsense! For the last time, please leave!

NIXON: Alright. Alright. I'm leaving. But I need to ask you one thing.

EMILY: Please go!

NIXON: One question, please.

EMILY: No!

J F K: Go, Nick!

NIXON: You've probably lost your concentration anyway. As soon as you left your writing table and came to the door. You're not in any mood to go back to that poem, that delicate sensation that sat in your hand like a baby sparrow before I knocked at the door. I saw it fly away. Fly away, sparrow! Fly away!

*(EMILY weeps.)*

NIXON: I know it's hard. I know. But if you would be kind enough to let me have another apple. For my brother. He doesn't get out very much. And if you could mention to my mother that I didn't ask for anything for myself. Just for my brother. Stop crying. Nobody would've read that poem anyway. But if you marry me, I'll see that you have all the privacy you want, to write as many poems as you want. Come on, stop that crying. One more lousy apple. And your hand in marriage.

J F K: Nick, you dog!

NIXON: Is it a deal?

*(She slowly closes the door on him.)*

NIXON: She likes me back! She likes me back! YOU'LL HAVE TO LOVE ME LOTS!

J F K: Nick, you old bow-wow! Good dog! Good dog!

NIXON: Bulldog! Bulldog! Bow-wow-wow! Just like school, huh, Jack? Bulldog! Bulldog! Bow-wow-wow!

J F K: That's Yale, Nick. I'm Crimson. *(He exits.)*

NIXON: Crimson! Maybe a little pink! She likes me back! Some would begrudge me my hard fought battle. They might say she's nothing to look at, she only gave you an apple, which you don't even like, and she only did it to send you away.

But she spoke to me. She answered the door, not once but twice. And when I come back, she'll recognize me. Isn't that something?

*(The radio comes on.)*

ANNOUNCER: And now stay tuned for another fun filled episode of *Amos 'n Andy...*

NIXON: I didn't turn the—Skippy?!?

ANNOUNCER: ...brought to you by the Committee to Elect Dwight D Eisenhower and Richard M Nixon!

NIXON: Ah-h-h-h-h!

*(The music comes up.)*

ANNOUNCER: We interrupt this broadcast to bring you a special news bulletin!

NIXON: Aw-w-w-w-w!

ANNOUNCER: General Dwight D Eisenhower announced today that he was considering dropping Senator Richard Nixon from the national ticket...

NIXON: Uh-h-h-h-h-h-h-h!

ANNOUNCER: ...because of rumors that Nixon has a secret slush fund and has accepted favors from private individuals, including a small dog for his daughter Tricia.

NIXON: Just a minute! He can't do that!

ANNOUNCER: He can do whatever he wants. He's General Eisenhower!

NIXON: Mommie!

ANNOUNCER: Your Mommie can't help you now.

NIXON: What am I going to do!

ANNOUNCER: Stay tuned for this broadcast.

(NIXON *turns the radio off.*)

(SKIPPY *appears.*)

SKIPPY: Bad news, Sir.

NIXON: Damn right, bad news.

SKIPPY: They caught Liddy, Sir. The President Apologizes to the Nation, take—

NIXON: We've got something more pressing, for crying out loud! The Senator Has to Explain It All to the American People! They want me to give up the dog!

(*Blackout*)

### END OF ACT ONE

# ACT TWO

*(The Oval Office)*

SKIPPY: Ladies and gentlemen: the First Lady of the United States.

EMILY: My fellow Americans: The heart asks pleasure first, and then, excuse from pain; and then, those little anodynes that deaden suffering. And then, to go to sleep; and then, if it should be the will of its Inquisitor, the liberty to die.

SKIPPY: You've cleared this with your husband?

EMILY: No.

SKIPPY: What do you think?

JEB: It's a downer, that part about "liberty to die."

SKIPPY: But she did say liberty.

JEB: Yeah. You haven't cleared this?

EMILY: No.

JEB: We could go with what I wrote.

SKIPPY: He won't say it. "Our fearful trip is done" is going to stick in his mouth. Either we go with her speech, or—

EMILY: The heart asks pleasure first, and then, excuse from pain—

JEB: Okay, okay.

EMILY: And then, those little anodynes that deaden suffering.

JEB: Thank you. We can run it by him, but—

EMILY: It's what the heart wants.

SKIPPY: Pain relief.

EMILY: Excuse from pain.

SKIPPY: Deadened suffering.

EMILY: It's what the heart asks.

JEB: Okay. I think we got it. Thank you.

EMILY: I think people should know. *(She exits.)*

JEB: I've been subpoenaed.

SKIPPY: What are you going to say?

JEB: I have to tell the truth. I did what they told me.

(NIXON *enters.*)

NIXON: I've got to make the speech of my life!

SKIPPY: That's right, Sir!

JEB: If you'll excuse me, Mr President: I've got to clear something with the Attorney General.

NIXON: Yeah, yeah, go on.

(JEB *exits.*)

NIXON: Like rats abandoning a sinking ship! Where are we, Skippy?

SKIPPY: Oval Office, Sir. Sir? I'm worried. If Liddy talks, what happens to me? I've got a family.

NIXON: Help me now, and your president will never desert you. Doesn't loyalty mean something around here?

SKIPPY: Sorry Sir, where were we?

NIXON: You were going to walk me around the goddamn set and make me look good.

SKIPPY: Yes, Sir. Okay, then. I've taken the liberty of drawing a circle on the floor, so if you want to get up and move around, we can keep a good shot.

NIXON: Good, good. And these are all my books?

SKIPPY: Yes, Sir.

NIXON: And my set.

SKIPPY: The Oval Office, Sir.

NIXON: A good set. Well, let's get started!

SKIPPY: Yes, Sir! The President Apologizes to the Nation! Take Eight!

NIXON: The year was 1952: Ike and the voters thought I'd amassed a secret fortune given to me by people who wanted to buy influence.

SKIPPY: No, Sir, Mr President!

(H R *enters.*)

H R: Just tell people the truth: where you got the money, and how you used it solely for campaign expenses.

NIXON: Right, right, but how's it going to look?

H R: This is the studio where they broadcast *This Is Your Life*. And this is the set the boys came up with, we call it "a G I bedroom den." Chair, table which will look like a desk, armchair you might want to put Mrs Nixon in.

NIXON: What's this piece of wood?

H R: Turn it around, Sir, you'll see it's a phony bookcase. These are your books, don't touch the titles, they're still wet.

NIXON: What's this one say? "Roosevelt Letters." Which Roosevelt?

H R: It's only a set, Sir. Now: there's the camera, and we want you to be natural.

NIXON: I can't do that.

H R: That's why we rehearse, Sir. To look natural.

NIXON: Get my wife, put her in the armchair. What's a candidate for high office without his wife? I want to feel where she is.

H R: She's on her way. As I was saying. We'll draw this circle on the floor, and we want you to stay inside the circle, so we can get a good picture.

NIXON: That's good.

H R: And we want you to keep it simple: sit at the table with your hands folded; then, get up and stand next to the table.

NIXON: Got it.

H R: Could we try it?

(NIXON *sits at the table, then stands next to it, then sits again.*)

H R: Good. Again?

(NIXON *stands at the table, then sits, then stands again.*)

NIXON: How's that?

H R: Remember, stay inside the circle. Now, let's try something with the hands: when you stand, put one hand on the table.

NIXON: Like this?

H R: Good. Then, take it off the table, and put the other one in your pocket.

NIXON: Stand at the table. One hand on the table, speak with the other.

H R: Right.

NIXON: Then put the speaking hand in the pocket, take the other off the table, and use that one to speak.

H R: That's all you have to do.

NIXON: Plus deliver the speech of my life.

(EMILY *enters.*)

H R: Okay, Mrs Nixon, in that chair. And all you have to do is strike a relaxed pose, turn your head a little more, smile, keep your eyes on your husband the whole time, and relax.
  Thirty seconds, Sir.

(NIXON *silently rehearses his blocking.*)

H R: Full disclosure, Sir. Just tell the truth.

NIXON: I just don't know if I can go through with this.

EMILY: Of course you can.

H R: Five...four...three...two...one.

NIXON: My fellow Americans. I come before you tonight as a candidate for the vice presidency and as a man whose honesty and integrity have been questioned.

SKIPPY: Take Eight!

NIXON: This is my life!

SKIPPY: Sir?

(ANNOUNCER *appears.*)

ANNOUNCER: Richard Milhous Nixon, THIS IS YOUR LIFE!

(*Applause from a studio audience.*)

ANNOUNCER: The year was 1952....

NIXON: I was wonderful in 1952.

SKIPPY: Sir?

ANNOUNCER: And you delivered the speech of a lifetime, what would come to be known as "The Checkers Speech." Do you remember this voice?

MOM: Now I want you to put on your best clothes, go to your one-room school house, and learn how hard and cruel life is....

NIXON: That's my dear mother!

(*Studio audience applauds.* MOM *comes out and embraces* NIXON.)

NIXON: I saw her suffer! Eat wax beans three times a day. My mother went to church on Easter Sunday, it was eighty-five degrees, and she never took her coat off, and do you know why?

ANNOUNCER: Why?

NIXON: Because she couldn't afford a dress. She was in her slip and stockings. I saw the perspiration form on her brow, and above her lip. And I held her hand tightly in mine. And my wool sweater didn't seem as warm as it did. Because that woman had courage.

ANNOUNCER: And then you met another woman who was very important in your life.

EMILY: I rose to your requirement, dropped the playthings of my youth.

NIXON: That's my wife, Pat!

(EMILY *embraces him. The studio audience applauds.*)

NIXON: She doesn't have a mink coat. But she does have a respectable cloth coat. And I always tell her that she'd look good in anything.

(*The studio audience applauds.*)

SKIPPY: Sir? It's 1973.

NIXON: Full disclosure. I took no money for personal use. Everybody had a secret fund, I wasn't the only one.

SKIPPY: Yes, Sir.

ANNOUNCER: And do you remember someone saying "Every penny I received was used to pay political expenses that I did not think should be charged to the taxpayers of the United States"?

NIXON: That was me!

(*The studio audience applauds as* NIXON *hugs himself.*)

NIXON: And when I stood at the table, put my hand in my pocket, and pulled out all the money I had on my person.
"My fellow Americans: I'm not a wealthy man. Look how much I've got on my person." (*He fishes in his pocket.*)
"A dollar. A quarter, two nickels... A dollar and forty-three cents. Pat, how much do you have on you? Would you check, please?"

EMILY: I have nothing.

NIXON: What about your good, Republican, cloth coat? Check your coat, dear. She's checking.

(*She checks.*)

EMILY: Fifty cents.

(*The studio audience applauds.*)

SKIPPY: Yes, Sir, but if we could try the apology—

NIXON: Then I took Tricia's piggy bank... "I have two youngsters—only the older one has any savings—and this isn't easy for me..." (*He breaks open the bank.*) "Let's see what she's got...those of you who might think I planned how much Pat and I would have on our persons couldn't possibly believe I know how much is in here...fifty, one dollar, dollar twenty, thirty... two dollars and fifty-three cents!"

SKIPPY: I don't remember that part, Sir.

ANNOUNCER: And do you remember this voice?

*(A dog barks.)*

NIXON: That me?

ANNOUNCER: No. A little hint? "...and the little cocker spaniel a man down in Texas sent us"?

NIXON: "The kids love that dog, and I just want to say this right now, that regardless of what they say about it, we're going to keep it."

*(The studio audience applauds.)*

ANNOUNCER: And this voice.

SKIPPY: Sir? Liddy's been indicted.

*(EMILY, MOM and the ANNOUNCER disappear.)*

NIXON: What?

SKIPPY: Liddy, Sir. For the break in.

NIXON: The hatchet? A petty, third-rate crime!

SKIPPY: Sir? I have a family, Sir. If Liddy talks...

*(LIDDY and JOHNNY appear.)*

LIDDY: Mr President? You wanted to see me?

NIXON: Mistakes were made, true. But I had the best interests of the country in mind when I did that.

LIDDY: When you chopped down that cherry tree, Mr President. It had to be done.

JOHNNY: It did not!

LIDDY: Hey, you little wimp, I should've killed you when I had the chance.

NIXON: Just a moment!

LIDDY: And you! Buck up, for Chrissakes! They're talking about you out there! Wandering the halls of the White House, drinking bourbon and mumbling to the pictures on the walls! Be a man worthy of your office!

NIXON: I'm trying!

LIDDY: Look in your own library, for God's sake! *(He pulls the Roosevelt letters book from the fake bookshelf.)* Teddy Roosevelt—and I quote: "I'm speaking for the man in the actual arena, whose face is marred by dust and sweat and blood, who strives valiantly, who errs, and comes up short again and again. Because there is not effort without error and shortcoming."

NIXON: I didn't chop down any tree! If I did, it would be wrong, but I didn't chop down any tree! You show me the hatchet.

LIDDY: I don't see any hatchet. Anyone see a hatchet?

SKIPPY: I just went over the transcript, Sir, and I don't see it anywhere.

LIDDY: That's the way it's going to be. *(He exits.)*

NIXON: What transcripts?

SKIPPY: The transcripts of the tapes. They found out that we tape everything, Sir, and the tapes have been subpoenaed.

NIXON: What about the *Amos 'n' Andy*? They get *Amos 'n' Andy*?

SKIPPY: Sir?

NIXON: I love *Amos 'n' Andy*! When I was a little boy—did I ever tell you this one?

SKIPPY: Yes, Sir.

NIXON: When I was a little boy, there was a little colored lad in our school, nobody liked him, either. So he and I sorta played together. Listened to the radio, at my father's store. He'd be Amos and I'd be Andy! Then we'd switch! He was better because he was the Real McCoy. But the one I dearly loved and identified with—what was the name of the other one? With the cigar? The one with the cigar, the real star.

SKIPPY: Kingfish?

NIXON: Kingfish! He wasn't even in the title! How we fought over who got to play the Kingfish! They can trust me, I loved the Kingfish!

SKIPPY: But Sir, I'm suggesting that if they look at the transcripts of the tapes—

NIXON: *(Turning the radio on)* I know what you're saying! If they get hold of the *Amos 'n Andy* we're dead! It's the Oval Office that's at stake. Leaders have to make the tough choices. Lincoln. Jefferson. My main man the Kingfish. He peddles his wife's tape to Dan Rather for the good of the Lodge, you know why? You wouldn't know, you never sat in this chair.

*(The scene shifts to the radio studio set.)*

ANNOUNCER: Return with us now to *The Amos 'n Andy Show*, brought to you by the Campaign to Make Dick Nixon President!

*(Music)*

*(SFX of a newsroom, DAN RATHER's office)*

DAN: Now let me get this straight, Mr Stevens. You've got a video tape of the assassination of President Abraham Lincoln?

KINGFISH: That's right, Mr Rather.

DAN: And you've seen it? What does it show?

KINGFISH: Of course I've seen it! It shows the great man watching the play, laughing his butt off during the comical parts. Then, wagging his foot and saying "get on, get on," during the sentimental portions. Then, it shows the killer sneaking into the booth.

DAN: John Wilkes Booth.

KINGFISH: How about that, Andy. The booth had a name!

ANDY: Kingfish, he's saying the name of the man that shot Lincoln.

KINGFISH: Oh, no. That's what the tape shows. Picture this: what did you say the name of the cat was, creeping into the booth?

DAN: Booth.

KINGFISH: Listen to this, Andy. The man wants us to believe Booth was in the booth. Mr Rather, I don't know what you take us for.

DAN: Does the tape clearly show Booth enter the booth?

KINGFISH: Damn right! This was taken with a Japanese camera; the highest quality!

DAN: And it clearly shows Booth shooting Lincoln?

KINGFISH: Hah! That's the fat part! It shows Booth in the booth, sneaking up. Lincoln laughing the part of his butt off that ain't already on the carpet. Sneaking up.

NIXON: Sneaking up!

KINGFISH: Sneaking up. Then, just when he's behind Mr Lincoln, he reaches into his coat pocket and pulls out a little script he'd written up for the occasion. It shows him emoting with wild gesture in the oratorical style of the time.

DAN: And it clearly shows him shoot Lincoln.

KINGFISH: I'm coming to that. The lights are low. The acting is fearsome. Booth don't like how his speech comes out, and he goes for his pen. He can't find a pen. He pulls a pistol, but he's looking for a pen. Booth goes out of the booth. Then, he comes back in the booth. He pulls out a pen. The suspense is so thick you could cut it up for sandwiches.

NIXON: Go, Kingfish!

ANDY: And then a young black cat pops out from behind the drapes, shoots Mr Lincoln in the coconut, pushes Booth out of the booth, onto the stage, and splits up the fire escape.

NIXON: Oh, Andy!

KINGFISH: Who's telling this story?

ANDY: I could see Mr Rather was getting impatient. Plus, we got to get to the ballpark.

DAN: This tape clearly shows a black man shoot President Lincoln?

KINGFISH: A relative of the Missus.

DAN: Naturally, I'd like to take a look at it.

KINGFISH: Well, naturally, I'd like you to. For a price.

NIXON: You tell him, Kingfish!

DAN: Mr Stevens. This is news. It would be unpatriotic to hold back important news like this for a few dollars.

KINGFISH: Hold on, now! We're talking family treasure! If you can't reach into your pockets and come out with more than a handful of lint, I just might hit up America's Funniest Home Videos.

DAN: Well, if it shows what you say it does, I'm sure we could come to some understanding.

KINGFISH: You'd best put your peepers on a diet, because this here tape is a feast for the eyes!

*(The radio goes off.)*

NIXON: Oh, poo! Where's the rest?

SKIPPY: Mr President, Sir?

NIXON: I lost the station! And this was the part where the network Jews the poor Kingfish down to practically nothing.

SKIPPY: Sir, maybe we could take another shot at that apology speech?

NIXON: You take a shot at it. Send Jeb in here!

SKIPPY: He's gone, Sir.

NIXON: Gone! Where did he go?

SKIPPY: Indicted, Sir.

NIXON: He should be in here covering my ass!

SKIPPY: I do know he's retained counsel, Sir. And recommended I do the same.

NIXON: He's going to turn on us, you watch. Cop a plea, get religion, and do community service.

SKIPPY: Jeb has your best interests at heart, Sir. Want to try that speech?

NIXON: I'm good on T V! I can make a case to the American People! ·

SKIPPY: Yes, Sir. Some makeup, Sir? Cover that five o'clock shadow?

NIXON: No! Roll the cameras. I'm ready for my close-up!

SKIPPY: The President Apologizes to the Nation...Take Nine!

NIXON: The year was 1960.

SKIPPY: Cut!

NIXON: No! Roll the cameras! I won that election fair and square. After eight years in Ike's dog house, I was ready! Me and Kennedy, *mano a mano*, in front of the voters for the whole enchilada!

*(The* ANNOUNCER *appears. J F K appears.)*

ANNOUNCER: It's the Presidential Debates, brought to you by—

NIXON: Just get on with it, I'm ready to play!

ANNOUNCER: Both of our finalists are ready: our first category is Good Citizenship, for the great states of Pennsylvania and New Jersey! Good Citizenship!

*(*NIXON *hits his bell.)*

ANNOUNCER: Vice President Nixon?

NIXON: It's time we stopped worrying about a free ride, I never got anything for nothing—

*(Booby buzzer. J F K hits his bell.)*

ANNOUNCER: Can you take it, Senator Kennedy?

J F K: Let me say this about that: Ask not what your country can do for you, but what you can do for your country.

*(Victory bell, and applause from the studio audience.)*

ANNOUNCER: That's right! And now, for California and Oregon, the category is Qualifications. Qualifications.

*(*NIXON *hits his bell.)*

ANNOUNCER: Mr Nixon! Qualifications.

NIXON: I've taken a lot of guff over the years—

*(Booby buzzer goes off. J F K hits his bell.)*

ANNOUNCER: I'm sorry. J F K?

J F K: The torch has been passed to a new generation!

*(Victory bell, and applause from the studio audience.)*

ANNOUNCER: That's right! And now, for the all important state of Illinois, and the right to be the next President of the United States.

*(J F K and* NIXON *hit their bells.)*

ANNOUNCER: I'm sorry, Mr Vice President! Jack?

J F K: My Daddy told me he'd buy me the election, but that he'd be damned if he was going to pay for a landslide!

*(Victory bell, laughter and applause from the studio audience.)*

*(*ANNOUNCER *and* J F K *vanish.)*

NIXON: I should've won that election. And I rode in that limousine. The one Kennedy was in. The Inauguration, 1960. I was vice president. It was a very cold day, and Eisenhower wasn't feeling well. There was still a chance we vice presidents dream about. In prize fights, they call it a puncher's chance—old Ike might step into the limo, grab his chest, keel over, and I would be President of the United States of America! For a lousy couple of minutes!

I was the defeated candidate in that limo, but I rode with my head held high, looking at the once and future presidents, hoping against hope that one would drop dead and the other would go away.

SKIPPY: Yes, Sir.

NIXON: Then I ran for governor, State of California. Lost there, too. You won't have Nixon to kick around anymore.

SKIPPY: Yes, Sir.

*(*NIXON *whines, whimpers, and gives a low moan.)*

*(An apple comes hurtling through the window.)*

NIXON: Protestors? They out there?

SKIPPY: That was a couple of years ago, Sir.

NIXON: Two rows of buses around the White House. There was great Civil War.

SKIPPY: Vietnam, Sir.

NIXON: Lincoln went among the men.

SKIPPY: Sir?

NIXON: The Civil War. He went among the men.

SKIPPY: He had a Civil War, Sir. You had civil unrest.

NIXON: I want to go out there and be among them.

SKIPPY: You did that, Sir. During the demonstrations. Right now it wouldn't be wise, Sir.

NIXON: If I could talk to them. If we went out there. And just talked. Lincoln did it.

SKIPPY: All due respect, Sir, that was different.

NIXON: But I can go out there. We're all Americans. I can talk to them!

*(A Civil War hospital)*

*(DAN'L lies dying. WALT enters.)*

WALT: Hello, brother. How's the Civil War going?

DAN'L: I'm dying.

WALT: I know.

DAN'L: Goddamn you! You ain't supposed to say that. You're supposed to tell me you're sorry. You wish it was you. You're gonna make it.

WALT: I'm here to help you.

DAN'L: You want to help? Run out and get me a woman.

WALT: Why?

DAN'L: Why! Are you stupid? So I don't die out, that's why! I only got a few minutes, and I ain't leaving the country to a bunch of fairies like you! Now go get me a woman while I yank up my willie. And a pretty one!

WALT: Maybe I can find someone to help you.

*(He exits and returns with HARRIET.)*

HARRIET: Stop the killing! End the war!

DAN'L: Hey, woman, hop aboard! I'm a veteran!

HARRIET: Bring the boys home!

DAN'L: I'm home and I'm horny. Now, climb on board before my flagpole goes to half mast. *(To WALT)* Talk some sense into her.

HARRIET: We're protesting the invasion of Cambodia.

DAN'L: Woman, cut the crap and jump my willie!

HARRIET: That's no way to talk to a woman, friend. Do you believe Mr Nixon is wrong to escalate the war?

DAN'L: No.

HARRIET: Goodbye.

DAN'L: Wait a minute! Come back! Yes! No! What's the right answer?

HARRIET: The answer is Yes. And what about all these Feds, taking our pictures and keeping secret files on us! Is that right?

DAN'L: No! Yes! No!

HARRIET: Nixon's screwing us, taking away our rights!

DAN'L: I'm losing it!

HARRIET: Is that right?

DAN'L: Yes! Yes! I'm dying already. This is my last hard-on! What do I got to do?

HARRIET: I'll pray for you!

DAN'L: Now wait just a goddamn minute! I thought you was one of them Make Love Not War types. He put you up to this?

(HARRIET *exits*.)

DAN'L: I've been screwed! I've been screwed!

WALT: Brother, please, this is no way to prepare—

(DAN'L *throttles* WALT.)

(NIXON *enters*.)

NIXON: I come in and walk among the troops, is that right? Pin a few medals, talk some football?

DAN'L: You son of a bitch! Goddamn hippie!

WALT: Help! Help!

DAN'L: I've been screwed! I've been screwed! I've been—

(DAN'L *dies*.)

(WALT *covers the body with a flag*.)

WALT: Purple Heart here, Sir.

NIXON: Huh! He didn't suffer much?

WALT: He suffered a lot, Sir.

NIXON: He died with an erection. Look at that thing!

WALT: An unfulfilled promise, Sir.

NIXON: I'll say. Wow! Any family?

WALT: Divorced.

NIXON: I'm not surprised. Look at that thing. (*Laughs*) I mean, could you imagine?

WALT: Lincoln never laughed at the dead.

NIXON: I'm not laughing. I'm not laughing.

SKIPPY: Do you want to take another shot at that apology speech? Walt could put it on the back of an envelope....

NIXON: No! Just leave me alone with the deceased. I won't laugh. Don't tell anyone I laughed.

WALT: Yes, Sir.

(WALT *exits.*)

NIXON: You didn't die in vain, friend.

DAN'L: The hell I didn't, if I'm leaving the country to a bunch of sissies like him.

NIXON: Who?

DAN'L: The liberals.

NIXON: The liberals.

DAN'L: They hounded me bad. I fought back, I mean, this is war. I was cut out for better things. I wanted to coach the Washington Redskins, right here in the capital.

NIXON: I love football!

DAN'L: That's what I like to hear. You aren't gonna be a scrub all your life.

NIXON: I was always just a little guy.

DAN'L: It ain't the size of the dog in the fight, Dick.

NIXON: It's the fight in the dog!

DAN'L: That's right. Don't let our kind of man disappear off the face of the continent. I'd've let you draw up plays, and send them to me.

NIXON: You'd run my plays?

DAN'L: I didn't say that. But I'd look at them. I know you're the president, but there are things more important.

NIXON: Football.

DAN'L: Brings men together. None of that sissy Kennedy touch, neither. It's war, Nixon. Don't trust anyone.

NIXON: Even your own team?

DAN'L: Get them before they get you.

NIXON: That's a fine erection you died with.

DAN'L: What good is it doing me? The last chance for America is in this pecker of mine. If I go, America goes with me. What about that hippie girl. Bring her back. Put her up here. Please? You're the president!

NIXON: Okay, Coach.

*(He exits and returns with* HARRIET.*)*

NIXON: She's messed up on drugs...whole generation, all on drugs.

HARRIET: Stop the killing! End the war!

DAN'L: Yeah, yeah. Just put her up there. Okay!

*(*NIXON *helps the drugged* HARRIET *mount* DAN'L.*)*

DAN'L: Oh, bless you, Richard Nixon!

*(*WALT *enters and watches, powerless.)*

NIXON: Walt, tell me something. When Lincoln died, people stood outside in the rain to see his coffin?

WALT: They waited through the night for his train to pass.

NIXON: How do you like that? Republican and Democrat?

WALT: They say that Lee himself wept.

NIXON: I've got a war. Nobody weeps for me. And they named a lot of things after him?

WALT: Lot of towns named Lincoln. They put him on a penny.

NIXON: Lincoln logs...I had some when I was a child. Not the full set, of course, they were hand-me-downs. Kennedy had a full set; each brother had a full set. I know this for a fact.

*(*HARRIET *comes to her senses and gets off* DAN'L.*)*

DAN'L: Wait a minute! What about my baby?

HARRIET: I'm on the pill! *(She exits.)*

DAN'L: Oh, sweet Jesus! We're leaving it all up to Nixon! *(He dies again.)*

WALT: Will that be all, Sir?

NIXON: No, no. I want to talk, man to man....

WALT: Go on.

NIXON: You don't like me very much, do you Walt?

WALT: No, Sir.

NIXON: Do you like football? Baseball? Little boys? Hah-hah, just joking. Do you like apples?

WALT: I love apples.

NIXON: I hate apples. We could get you apples, all the apples you want. But it would be wrong! Would you like an apple?

WALT: Maybe later, Sir.

NIXON: Lincoln liked apples?

WALT: He loved apples.

NIXON: Me, too. Me, too, Walt. I love apples. My mother loved apples. She did. Loved them.
  They stood in the rain. A warm rain?

WALT: It was April. It was a cold, hard rain.

NIXON: I'd like to flip the coin that starts the Super Bowl someday. Lincoln ever do that?

WALT: No, Sir.

NIXON: Well, maybe if he did, they wouldn't have to stand in the rain to have a peak at him. Did he like football?

WALT: I think there are more important matters before us, Sir.

NIXON: This is important! Binding the nation's wounds! Man to man, how are we going to bind the nation's wounds?

WALT: There's a cancer on the presidency, Sir. It would help if you apologized for what you did. Otherwise, presidents from now through the next century are going to have one heck of a credibility problem.

NIXON: And that would be my fault?

WALT: Yes, Sir. That would be your legacy.

NIXON: Then, let's do it.

(WALT *nods to* SKIPPY.)

(*The Oval Office.*)

SKIPPY: The President Apologizes to the Nation... Take Ten: Three. Two. One.

NIXON: Wait a minute.

SKIPPY: What's wrong, Sr?

NIXON: Where's the tape?

SKIPPY: What tape, Sir?

NIXON: The part of *The Amos 'n' Andy* show where Sapphire and her Mama are in the cab, and Amos makes a big speech how he's glad Sapphire's ancestor got Whitey. Then the women discover their tape is missing.

SKIPPY: Seems to have been erased, Sir.

NIXON: That's illegal!

SKIPPY: I wouldn't know, I'm not an attorney, Sir, but it's gone.

NIXON: Where's MacGruder?

SKIPPY: Indicted, Sir.

NIXON: Indicted! What about Haldeman?

SKIPPY: I'm not sure, Sir. Mr President, Sir?

NIXON: What is it, Skippy!

SKIPPY: Sir. That's Liddy, Sir, indicted. MacGruder, Sir, indicted. Then there's Colson, he's subpoenaed: I don't know what he knows or what he's prepared to testify.

NIXON: What's the problem?

SKIPPY: I'm worried about my own self, Sir. If I'm indicted...

NIXON: You won't be indicted, Skippy.

SKIPPY: I have a family, Sir. I've always tried to do right by you.

NIXON: I know, Skippy, and I reward loyalty. Loyalty, tenacity, dogged perseverance. Why do you think they elected me president? Because they liked me?

SKIPPY: No, Sir.

NIXON: They knew I wouldn't appear on a penny. Have any bridges named after me. Tunnels. They just set me up to knock me down. And I'm president, for crying out loud. Nothing!

SKIPPY: You've done nothing wrong.

ANNOUNCER: And now for the conclusion of tonight's *Amos 'n' Andy Show*. brought to you by CREEP, The Committee to Re-Elect the President.

NIXON: Goodie!

*(SFX of a fish fry. Music, lots of voices.)*

LODGE BROTHER: Hey, Kingfish, this is some fish fry. Where's the fish?

KINGFISH: Now hold on, fellow Lodge members. How's about a little respect for getting Jackie Robinson to the Mystic Knights of the Sea Fish Fry?

ANDY: But Kingfish, there ain't no Jackie Robinson. And there ain't no fish.

KINGFISH: Don't be held up in the technicalities, Andy. When Dan Rather gets here with the money for the tape, everything is going to work out. Look at this baseball. Jackie Robinson hit me this ball in the ninth inning.

NIXON: How much proof do you need, for Christ's sake?

ANDY: Kingfish, Jackie Robinson didn't hit that ball to you. You pulled it out of the hands of a little child.

KINGFISH: The child should've been in school!

NIXON: You tell them!

NORTON: Oh, Mr Kingfish.

KINGFISH: Oh, Mr Norton, how can I help you.

NORTON: I need the money you owe me for renting this hall.

KINGFISH: How much we talking here?

NORTON: It could be as much as a million.

NIXON: One million? No problem.

KINGFISH: The money's on the way.          ·

NIXON: But it would be wrong!

KINGFISH: Andy! Hey, Andy! What time's Jackie Robinson showing up?

ANDY: I was just going to ask you the same question.

KINGFISH: You talked to him.

ANDY: I thought you did!

KINGFISH: Andy, listen here: why do you think I gave you that yellow piece of paper with instructions? Pick up all the napkins at the ball park; collect all the paper cups in the bleachers; and, talk to Jackie Robinson!

ANDY: You didn't give me any list.

KINGFISH: I had the list right here, on a yellow piece of paper stuck in my hat band, so I'd remember to give it to you.

ANDY: It was a yellow piece of paper sticking in your hat band?

KINGFISH: That's right.

ANDY: On the left hand side.

KINGFISH: That's right.

ANDY: Hope you had two, 'cause one's still up there.

KINGFISH: What?

*(SFX paper shuffled)*

KINGFISH: Oh, my!

KINGFISH/NIXON: Oh my-my-my. What is going to become of the Kingfish?

AMOS: Hey, Kingfish!

KINGFISH: Howdy, Amos.

AMOS: I've just seen Sapphire and her Mama, and they're heading this way. Listen here, Kingfish, there is a cancer on the Mystic Knights of the Sea—

NIXON: Uh-oh...

ANDY: I can get to it with this hatchet. *(He wields the cherry tree hatchet.)*

NIXON: I thought I told you to get rid of that hatchet!

KINGFISH: Ha-ha. That ain't my hatchet!

NIXON: You tell them, Kingfish!

ANDY: Look out, Kingfish, here they come.

NIXON: Uh-oh!

SAPPHIRE: George Stevens! What's this I hear about you stealing my family tape so you and your Lodge Brothers can eat fish?

KINGFISH: Oh, honey, I'm glad you stopped—

SAPPHIRE: Don't you Oh honey me, you thief! You liar! You think you can sweet talk your way out of this one—

MAMA: Not while I'm around, honey child.

NIXON: Judge and jury!

KINGFISH: Hello, Mama.

MAMA: I told you this was a size three head in a size ten hat when you married him. He sold the whole Negro race down the river for a Fish Fry!

DAN: Excuse me, Mr Stevens?

SAPPHIRE: Mama! It's Dan Rather!

NIXON: We've got to get rid of that hatchet!

KINGFISH: Yes, Sir!

DAN: I'm sorry, Mr Stevens, but regarding that tape of yours. We looked at it very carefully, and I'm afraid it doesn't show what you claim.

KINGFISH: What does it show?

DAN: It's a recording of high crimes and misdemeanors committed in the Oval Office.

KINGFISH: But it shows the dude leap up and—

NIXON: It what?!?

DAN: And we expect that the Supreme Court will order the release of all the tapes, so we hope to get to the bottom of this.

NIXON: Dan Rather has the tape!

DAN: Mr Stevens, let me give you some advice.

NIXON: Dan Rather has the tape!

DAN: Resign your office as president of The Mystic Knights of the Sea. Before you're impeached. And that's our world. Goodnight.

NIXON: Skippy!

(NIXON *turns the radio off.* SKIPPY *appears.*)

SKIPPY: Sir?

NIXON: We did it to protect the Lodge.

SKIPPY: Sir?

NIXON: The Lodge, for Chrissakes! Skippy, you've got to get rid of this tape!

SKIPPY: I can't do that, Sir.

NIXON: I'm giving you an Executive Order, for crying out loud!

SKIPPY: I'll go to jail, Sir.

NIXON: Someone's got to—what would the Kingfish do?

SKIPPY: I have a family, Sir.

NIXON: That's it! There's still hope. Get the First Lady down here.

SKIPPY: She won't come down, you said yourself.

NIXON: *(Hitting the intercom)* Dear, could you come down a moment? I've decided to leave public life and return to California.
      It's a little game we play.

(EMILY *appears.*)

EMILY: Oh, Richard!

NIXON: She moves when she wants to. Dear, we need a favor. If you could come sit here in my chair for a moment. Don't worry, we're here. And look into the camera. And explain to our fellow Americans how you erased the tape.

EMILY: I hate you.

NIXON: It was an honest mistake, you were writing your poetry, you thought you had some ideas you'd put on tape—

EMILY: I hate you.

NIXON: And maybe leaned over while you were typing—it's a little awkward, but with a little practice.

EMILY: I hate you.

NIXON: We need it tonight, dear.

EMILY: Will there really be a morning?

NIXON: You can trust me.

*(She exits.)*

NIXON: Dear? *(He turns on the radio.)* Oh, what's to become of the Kingfish?

AMOS: Like I say, Kingfish, there is a cancer on the Presidency. But if you want to do the right thing—

SKIPPY: Sir?

(NIXON *turns the radio off.*)

NIXON: What is it!

SKIPPY: I've been indicted for withholding evidence. My lawyer says I'm going to be subpoenaed to appear before the Select Committee. My mother in Illinois, when she sees me on T V—

NIXON: What about your mother?

SKIPPY: What should I do?

NIXON: I could protect you, Skippy. But it would be wrong. Did you get that on tape? It would be wrong.

SKIPPY: Maybe, Mr President, if you can't apologize to them, could you apologize to me?

NIXON: For what?

SKIPPY: I did what you told me.

NIXON: So did Liddy. And Haldeman. MacGruder. My wife did everything I asked her to! And my mother. My mother was a saint!

SKIPPY: Maybe, Sir, when I testify and plead guilty and go to prison for doing what you told me—

NIXON: What?

SKIPPY: I'll feel better knowing you meant me no harm. It's what I believed.

NIXON: Well, you shouldn't have. You shouldn't trust anyone. Because they'll let you down. Are we done?

SKIPPY: Yes, Sir. Good night, Sir. Pleasant dreams. (*He exits.*)

NIXON: Wait a minute, Skippy, for God's sake, you're not going to leave your president! Jeez Louise, I can't apologize. I'm the Kingfish! (*He turns the radio on.*)

ANDY: Hey, Kingfish, here comes that Mr Norton, looking for his hundred dollars. The way I see it, there's only one way out.

KINGFISH: What's that?

ANDY: You got to apologize to the people you done wrong.

NIXON: He can't apologize! He's the Kingfish!

(JACKIE ROBINSON *appears.*)

JACKIE: Excuse me...

ANDY: It's Jackie Robinson, in the flesh!

JACKIE: Excuse me. I was on my way home from the ballpark when I encountered a bit of car trouble.

AMOS: I can fix that! Mr Robinson, let me have a look at it!

JACKIE: Why, that's very kind of—say, is that catfish I smell?

ANDY: It sure is.

NIXON: We're screwed!

JACKIE: Why, I just love fried fish!

ANDY: Want to join us?

JACKIE: I couldn't....

ANDY: Please, Mr Robinson, the Mystic Knights of the Sea would be honored.

JACKIE: If you insist...say, is that the ball I hit for a home run to win the game today?

KINGFISH: This collar's getting a little tight....

NIXON: The room a little small...

ANDY: It sure is!

JACKIE: I could've sworn a child caught it, but I'll give you a hundred dollars if I can have it back. And box seats for everyone here to see our next game.

KINGFISH: What's the catch?

NIXON: Don't agree to anything!

JACKIE: All you have to do is apologize to all the people who trusted you—

NIXON: Don't do it, Kingfish!

JACKIE: —and resign your presidency of the Mystic Knights of the Sea Lodge.

NIXON: No!

ANDY: Better do what he says, Kingfish.

AMOS: It removes the cancer from the presidency.

NIXON: What if he gives the ball back, and promises never to do it again?

JACKIE: No, I'm afraid he has to resign.

KINGFISH: Apologize for trying to do right by my Lodge?

SAPPHIRE: And double-crossing your own wife? I hate you!

NIXON: That's a little strong, dear.

JACKIE: Apologize and step down.

NIXON: Wait just a minute!

KINGFISH: I'm sorry, Sapphire. I'm sorry, boys. I done a terrible thing, and I'm unfit to be president of this here Lodge.

ANDY: And Jackie, maybe you'd like to be our new Lodge president.

JACKIE: I'd be honored!

NIXON: Oh, treachery! You did it to protect the Lodge! Oh, why did you back down, Kingfish? (*He turns the radio off.*)

(KINGFISH *appears in the Oval Office.*)

KINGFISH: Why, I seen the handwringing on the wall and figured it was time to cut and run!

NIXON: Good God, you're white!

KINGFISH: You've only seen me on the radio.

NIXON: You're white, I can't believe it!

KINGFISH: No time for that now, Tricky. If I were you, I'd step aside till this thing cools down. Then, when they see you in a new light, you'll be back quicker than they can say Jack Robinson! Hah-hah!

NIXON: You tricked us! You were my colored pal, a credit to your race!

KINGFISH: They figured the same thing about you.

NIXON: I've been duped. You lied to me!

KINGFISH: Get real, Nixon!

NIXON: You pretended you were black!

KINGFISH: Just told a little white lie, that's all.

NIXON: Then, you apologized.

KINGFISH: Oh, yeah. I apologized. Sorry, folks! Had my fingers crossed.

(*They cackle.*)

KINGFISH: I can see you ain't learned nothing!

NIXON: I'm eager to learn! What about the tapes? Dan Rather has the tapes!

(KINGFISH *holds up the tapes.*)

KINGFISH: I pulled the old switcheroo!

NIXON: He got the poke! We got the pig!

(KINGFISH *gives* NIXON *the tapes.*)

KINGFISH: You want anything done right around here, you have to do it yourself.

NIXON: Let me have it. *(He erases the tapes.)*

KINGFISH: Hey, I'm getting erased!

NIXON: Sorry about that! *(He laughs.)* How's that for an apology? Sorry the tape got erased! Sorry there's no smoking gun!

*(KINGFISH fades away.)*

KINGFISH: So long, Tricky!

NIXON: Goodbye, Kingfish! Goodbye old friend!
    The son of bitch was white! How do you like— If he could pull that off...
    It's the fight in the dog, not the dog in the fight....
    Skippy? Skippy?!
    Oh, for crying out loud, anything you want done, you have to do it—
    Cameras rolling? I'm ready for my closeup.
    My fellow Americans...as of three P M today, I hereby resign my office as President of the United States of America.
    Still rolling? If I may be allowed a personal moment. We don't have a good phrase for for it in English, but the French have an expression on occasions like this. *Au revoir! Au revoir!* Which doesn't translate exactly. It's more than goodbye. More than farewell. It means that someday, when this is over, don't know when, I'll be back!
    Thank you and good night!

*(Blackout)*

END OF PLAY

# BROADWAY PLAY PUBLISHING INC

## ONE ACT COLLECTIONS

### THE COLORED MUSEUM

### ENSEMBLE STUDIO THEATER MARATHON `84

### FACING FORWARD

### GIANTS HAVE US IN THEIR BOOKS

### ONE ACTS AND MONOLOGUES FOR WOMEN

### ORCHARDS

### ORGASMO ADULTO ESCAPES FROM THE ZOO

### PLAYS BY LOUIS PHILLIPS

### ROOTS IN WATER

### SHORT PIECES FROM THE NEW DRAMATISTS

### WHAT A MAN WEIGHS &
### THE WORLD AT ABSOLUTE ZERO

# BROADWAY PLAY PUBLISHING INC

## PLAYWRIGHTS' COLLECTIONS

### PLAYS BY NEAL BELL
MCTEAGUE: A TALE OF SAN FRANCISCO
RAGGED DICK
THÉRÈSE RAQUIN

### PLAYS BY ALAN BOWNE
BEIRUT
FORTY-DEUCE
SHARON AND BILLY

### PLAYS BY LONNIE CARTER
LEMUEL
GULLIVER
GULLIVER REDUX

### PLAYS BY STEVE CARTER
DAME LORRAINE
HOUSE OF SHADOWS
MIRAGE
ONE LAST LOOK
TEA ON INAUGURATION DAY

### PLAYS BY ANTHONY CLARVOE
LET'S PLAY TWO
THE LIVING
SHOW AND TELL

### PLAYS BY DONALD FREED
ALFRED AND VICTORIA: A LIFE
CHILD OF LUCK
IS HE STILL DEAD?

### PLAYS BY ALLAN HAVIS
HOSPITALITY
MINK SONATA
MOROCCO

### PLAYS BY ALLAN HAVIS, VOLUME TWO
A DARING BRIDE
THE LADIES OF FISHER COVE
SAINTE SIMONE

# BROADWAY PLAY PUBLISHING INC

## TOP TEN BEST SELLING
## FULL-LENGTH PLAYS AND
## FULL-LENGTH PLAY COLLECTIONS

BATTERY

THE IMMIGRANT

NATIVE SPEECH

ONE FLEA SPARE

ON THE VERGE

PLAYS BY TONY KUSHNER
(CONTAINING A BRIGHT ROOM CALLED DAY,
THE ILLUSION, & SLAVS!)

PRELUDE TO A KISS

THE PROMISE

TALES OF THE LOST FORMICANS

TO GILLIAN ON HER 37TH BIRTHDAY